The
Givenness
of
Things

Sermons and Reflections of Father James A. Callahan

Rector, St.Margaret's Episcopal Church 1982-2000

Lisa Plummer Crafton

Vabella Publishing
P.O. Box 1052
Carrollton, Georgia 30112
www.vabella.com

Manufactured in the United States of America

Library of Congress Control Number: 2014900079

13-digit ISBN 978-1-938230-67-7

10 9 8 7 6 5 4 3 2 1

This book is dedicated to the Callahan family,

to Peg, Mary, Susan, Martha, and to the memory of John.

Acknowledgements

I am thankful to Rev. Hazel Glover of St. Margaret's for her support and encouragement in this project but even more so for her loving spirit that infuses this parish family and makes it the beautiful, warm home that it is for so many of us.

I am thankful to generous donors who have made the publication possible, especially Fred and Anne Richards, Robert Claxton, Sue Medeiros, and Bruce Bobick.

I am thankful to Catherine Gordon, the director of St. Margaret's Outreach, and to all who serve in Outreach in this church community, who carry on the work that was closest to Jim's heart by living out our reputation as "the church that helps people."

I am especially grateful for the love and support of my family, to my best friend and husband Micheal with whom I have the wonderful good fortune to have been close friends with Jim Callahan for almost twenty years and to my children Elizabeth and Will who carry memories of Jim from their childhood.

Table of Contents

Foreward

For the last two years, I have been honored to live immersed in the words of Jim Callahan, that larger-than-life poet priest of Irish descent, who served as Rector of St. Margaret's Episcopal Church in Carrollton, Georgia from 1982-2000. Transcribed from audio cassette tapes as well as typed and handwritten copies of sermons that I treasure, these words are a tangible, permanent record of Jim's reflections on the gospel—not understood in terms of general principles of theology or philosophy, but in the way we as humans experience it: the gospel that is "gotten at" in a community of people, spontaneous laughter over a drink at a kitchen table, or at Jerry's Country Kitchen over coffee and biscuits, or tears shared over a grave. His is a theology of incarnation, of the way that the trinity of joy, sorrow, and love is the story of our life, of the fact that our human life on earth is not a journey to Paradise but rather *is* Paradise. The title of this collection echoes a phrase that comes up many times in these pages and which speaks to our willingness to embrace the joy and the sorrow and love of which we live in the midst.

As Jim puts it, "For apart from that world—the *givenness* of things—you and I have no being and make no sense. For it is just the *givenness* of things—this sadness and sorrow, this all too fleeting pleasure, this boredom and fear and terror, and this laughter and these tears—that are the *thick of it* into, or out of which God speaks."

Those of us who experienced Jim's words behind a pulpit know of their power, how week after week he took a gospel passage that might have seemed a bit dull, a ribbon that had lost its sheen with too much handling, and pulled that ribbon into the fabric of a sermon where the meaning would suddenly shine forth, as one of Jim's favorite poets Gerard Manley Hopkins would say, in "God's Grandeur," "like shining from shook foil." But, even more importantly, the power of the message lives out there in all those who encountered Jim wherever he happened to be—from the clerk who sold him his peanut butter crackers at the gas station, to the waitresses at Millie's, to the pizza delivery boy stunned by Jim's outrageously generous tip, to a taxi driver in Durham, England who would go on to become a priest himself, inspired by the gift of Jim's friendship.

Jim's words are layered with others' words, so we hear in these pages words of wisdom from theological figures, from Diedrich Bonhoeffer to his favorite Episcopal writer Frederich Buechner. His sermons are infused with lyrical words of others, from literary allusions to Shakespeare's Caliban of *The Tempest*, Dickens' Ebenezer Scrooge, the lyrics of Robert Frost and Thomas Hardy and John Donne, the novels of Alice Walker and Cormac McCarthy, to American cultural treasures like *The Wizard of Oz* or the gospel of St. James, Sweet Baby James Taylor, that is. But, perhaps the most powerful voices here come from the characters Jim loved to talk about, his notorious Uncle Henry and Aunt Sue Belle and Mama Jesse and, of course, his own mother whom he immortalized in his labeling of John the Baptist as "my mother in drag," and the fictional apostle Jim created, the very Jewish Murray who shows up asking very human questions, not having gotten the memo of where he was supposed to be!

It is these stories through which God speaks, not stories about God's doctrines or the church, but a God who outrageously really loves us, who, as Jim says, "gives himself generously and with abandon, like some crazy sower who throws seeds everywhere, like some crazy father who forgives his Prodigal Son everything under the sun just for the joy of having him home again," a God Jim likened to a commercial about Crazy Eddie's Auto Sales, that Crazy Eddie God of ours whose low prices are just ridiculous!

As a collection of sermons, it is, of course, incomplete. I often run into people who say "Do you have the one about . . . ?" Those have a vibrant life of their own through oral storytelling. One in particular is Jim's recollection of what he called the best Easter sermon he'd ever heard, given by a local African-American preacher, who got at the essence of God's love: "It's like you be cryin' and there ain't nobody died; you be laughing, and nobody told a joke; you be running, and ain't nobody chasing you."

Finally, the words here bid us to remember, to remember all those who came before us and touched us and were Jesus to us in ways we often overlook. As Jim puts it, "We need each other. You can survive on your own. You can grow strong on your own. You can even prevail on your own, but you cannot, I think, become fully human on your own."

In collecting and offering these words, then, we remember Jim's ministry. And memory is not nostalgia but an active reclaiming: "Memory is more than a looking back to a time that is no longer. It's a looking deep into another kind of time altogether, where everything that ever was continues not just *to be*, but to grow and change with a life that's in it still. The people we loved. The people who loved us. The people who taught us things. Dead and gone though they may be, as we come to understand them in new ways, it's as though they come to understand us, and *through them*, we come to understand ourselves in new ways too."

The book opens with a sermon Jim preached out in Montana about coming home to Georgia and what that meant, and it ends with the final sermon he did on his last Sunday at St. Margaret's. In between, there are multiple sermons about some of the same gospel passages (John the Baptist and Advent, the feeding of the five thousand), and I have grouped these together so readers can enjoy the different lenses through which he talked about the same topic. Otherwise, the ordering of the sermons is mine—a rhythm of tones, moods, messages, and life stories that take readers into the "givenness of things."

Lisa Plummer Crafton

Come Unto Me

"Come unto me, all ye who labor, and are heavy laden
. . . and I will give you rest. Take my yoke upon you, and
learn of me; for I am gentle and lowly of heart, and you will
find rest for your soul. For my yoke is easy, and my burden
is light."

To what sort of weariness does Jesus speak? And to
what sort of burden? Is it a word of comfort to old
pilgrims—the discount of grace given to senior citizens or
battle-weary saints? I think not. I think rather that he
speaks to whatever *weariness there is* in whoever his hearers
are. To whatever it is in you and me that *listens* and *hears*. I
believe that he speaks as much to the weariness that comes
when our hearts are broken and our dreams shattered in
growing up as he does to the fatigue and despair that sets in
when we have grown old. I believe that he speaks to what
grows old before its time in the youngest of us—faith and
hope and love—and which must be resurrected every day of
our lives if it is to remain fresh and alive and real.

I recall my encounter with a shattered looking youth
in Central City Park. "What's wrong," I asked. "Everything,"
he said. "Are you all right?" "No." "Can I help?" "Probably
not."

As I mentioned to you before, I came to Montana
with an old Boy Scout need of mine to recognize and be
able to identify many of the trees that grow so wondrously
in this great region. To the embarrassment of my family, I
think, I took on all the postures of Tommy Tourist with my
little manual in hand, checking out needles and leaves and

bark. You see, before I came out here, I was like that lovely Welsh poet, Dylan Thomas, at least in this one respect: "All trees are oaks—except elms; all birds are swans—except geese; all flowers are roses—except chrysanthemums." If you were of a cynical mind, you could say of me what one of my English professors said of the eighteenth-century Romantic poets. He called them "city-spawned youth who went slumming through Nature."

Well, whatever. I simply wanted to know their names. And now that I am leaving, I want them to know mine. Or assuming that trees don't go in much for naming things, at least to know that someone with my ordinary name and less than memorable face stood in awe of them, wondered at them and felt humbled in their presence, and will remember them forever.

Come unto me, all ye who labor . . . and I will give you rest. I will give you the oaks and the elms, the tamaracks and the firs, the spruces, and the beautifully shimmering leaves of the aspen who dance for their sister, the *wind*.

Since I have been here, I have thought a great deal about a speech of Caliban's in Shakespeare's *The Tempest*. Half monster and madman that he is, he tells two of the shipwrecked survivors who people this lovely play, who are washed miraculously upon the shore of Prospero's magical island, this. Caliban says to them, in Act 3, scene 2:

> "Be not afeard. The isle is full of noises, sounds, and
> sweet airs that give delight and hurt not. Sometimes
> a thousand twangling instruments will hum about
> mine ears. And sometimes voices that if I then had

waked after long sleep will make me sleep again.
And then, in dreaming, clouds methought would
open and show riches ready to drop upon me, that
when I waked, I cried to dream again."

"Be not afeard."

But now we go home to our own island, with its own
noises, sounds, and sweet airs that give delight and hurt not.
To hills and mountains not so majestic as yours, to summer
mornings not so cool and invigorating as yours, and to oaks
and elms and pines not quite so tall or stately as your
towering evergreens. But, I suppose that the things in them
that call us back, make us even hungry and yearning to
return, is that whatever their own special beauty is, or
whatever beauty they lack, they are, after all, *our* hills and
mountains, *our* fields and streams; they are our children and
parents and friends and adversaries. In a simple word, they
are *home*. Not too different, I suspect, from the houses to
which you return every day—from your labor and from
your being heavy-laden.

"Home," as Robert Frost says, in "The Death of a
Hired Man," "is the place where, when you have to go
there, they have to take you in."

Come unto me, all ye that labor—and I will give you
home. Not just a heavenly one, either, if you're lucky. An
earthly, incarnate one—where there's always something to
be fixed, always something wearing out, always taxes to be
paid, where there's sometimes as much laboring as being
heavy-laden, as much agonizing and unrest on the inside as

there is on the outside, maybe even more. But home it is, nevertheless.[1]

And he calls us as much to that home as he does to the heavenly one, and our journey to it and in it and through it is as sacred and shot-through with meaning as our journey to Paradise. *It is, my dear friends, our journey to Paradise.*

It's like Caliban's little island home—full of noises, sounds, and sweet airs that give delight and hurt not. It's a place, for me at least, where there are books to be read and poems to write, and people to love; where there is grass to cut, and a living to earn, and neighbors to care for and fuss with, and things to be gloriously put off till tomorrow . . . or never! And things to be put *on*, and risks to run and losses to suffer. And if we're lucky, little victories to be won.

But there are other noises, too—noises, sounds, and not-so-sweet airs that give no delight and hurt like hell. Someone we love suffers. Someone we adore and depend on dies. And as Mark Twain says, "When someone you love dies, it's like when your house burns down. It's years before

---

[1]In alternate notes for this sermon, Jim added here,
"A self to be, other selves to love and work to do, but when we have found that, we discover that there is also something crucial missing which we have not found and search for that too. . . . My stay here has been at a time in my life in which this quest, this sacred and foot-sore journey, has been or is being greatly renewed. . . . What I have not found, I cannot name, and for the most part know of only through my sense of its precious and puzzling and haunting absence. And maybe we, all of us, can never name it by its final, true, and holy name. And maybe it's largely through its absence that, this side of Paradise, we will ever know it.

you realize the full extent of your loss." We fail a friend. Or a friend fails us. And we're appalled at the capacity we all of us share for estranging the very people in our lives that we need the most.

Or maybe nothing extraordinary happens at all. Just one day following another, helter-skelter in the manner of days. We sleep, we dream, we wake, we work, we remember, and we forget. We have fun, and we are depressed. We laugh, and we get fed up.

I saw a crazy T-shirt in one of your gift shop windows the second day we were here. Below a picture of what looked like a medieval version of one of the Rolling Stones, it said, "I don't like glaciers. I don't like Park Rangers. I don't like grizzlies. And I'm not crazy about you, either, Pal." If I hadn't known it before, I knew then that I was going to love Whitefish [the town in Montana] if for no other reason than there was somebody here as crazy and sick as I was!

It's part of the *givenness of things*, that makes us one with park rangers and grizzlies, so that we can laugh at each other and at ourselves, at the park ranger in all of us who likes to tell people where to go and what to see, and at the grizzly in all of us that would devour and wipe out the whole township for a taste of honey or an unmolested feast at some garbage dumps!

It's the humbling knowledge that when we are at our most dazzling, there's always *somebody* who's not too crazy about us, either, Pal!

To simply despise that is to despise the world that God died to save. It is, in fact, to despise yourself and your own incarnation. For apart from that world—the *givenness* of things—you and I have no being and make no sense. For it is just the *givenness* of things—this sadness and sorrow, this all too fleeting pleasure, this boredom and fear and terror, and this laughter and these tears—that are *the thick of it into, or out of* which God speaks.

"God chose what is foolish in the world to shame the wise. God chose what is weak in the world to shame the strong. God chose what is lonely and despised, even things that are not, to put to nought the things that are" [I Corinthians 1: 26-31].

The foolish shaming the wise puts me in mind of some others of God's natural creatures, crows and larks. There is a wonderfully courageous—and somewhat comic—little scenario that gets frequently played out in Nature. You can see it along highways, usually in open fields. When a bird of prey, like a hawk, or an otherwise mischievous, large bird, like a crow, flaps his winged way through the domain of other smaller and less malevolent birds, most of them scatter and take cover wherever they can. But a few species are not so easily intimidated, in my part of the country, mockingbirds and kingfishers. They flit along always above the invader, and with great audacity dive down and peck him on the top of his head—this to a creature ten times their size, this to a creature who carries sudden death in its talons or its sharp beak. They never seriously damage the great bird. But they give him quite more than his share of consternation, goading him out of their territory to more friendly and unperturbed skies.

Well, I have seen this little air show a thousand times in my life, I guess, and have delighted—even wondered—at each one. Such courage! Such audacity! But never before had I seen it played out to the end, or rather, to an intermission until I came here to Montana. I was coming back from taking my son John to the airport. The sun was just above the mountain as I drove into town by way of Dillon Road. A huge, black crow was doing his early morning, lazy reconnaissance across a misty field, when the dive bombers flew into action. There must have been five or six of them—sparrows or larks, or whatever they were—making that old bird wish he had stayed in bed or that he had picked some other field. He soared low, just above the ground, and finally came to rest on the post of a barbed-wire fence, struggling, I suppose, to regain his composure. To my amazement and great laughter, his assailants called off the attack and came to rest on the same barbed-wire fence, not two feet from the crow. There they all sat for a few moments, the old crow shaking out his much battered head and the larks, or whatever, preening themselves or checking for lice, or whatever larks check for. They all looked like a group of *chums* sitting around a bar rail, the crow the oddest member of the bunch! Then, after a moment's respite, the crow took off again, and the battle resumed until they all flew out of sight as if in an airplane commercial: "Delta is ready when you are."

I rode on into town laughing awhile—and then wondering if the crow would miss the larks if they weren't around, as I was beginning already to miss my son. Or if the larks ever grow lonely for the crow.

I went back to my rectory, and while my wife and daughter slept, I wrote it all down. It was one of the things I had come up here to Montana to see, without knowing it. God sent ahead of my coming to prepare—as one finds rooms made ready for one's lodging.

You see, we can survive on our own, we can grow strong on our own, but we cannot become human on our own. Let us call it God's *declaration of interdependence.*

That's why, I think, in Jesus' sad joke, the rich man has as hard a time getting into Paradise as the camel—because with his checkbooks in his pocket, the rich man is so effective at getting everything he needs that he doesn't see that the thing he needs most can be had only as a gift.

Come unto me, all ye that labor—and I will give you each other.

John the Baptist I

"In those days came John the Baptist, preaching in the wilderness of Judea, 'Repent, for the kingdom of heaven is at hand...'"

And what are the words that pierce our hearing and disturb our hearts? The *wilderness*—repent—a coat of camel's hair—a leather girdle—locusts and wild honey—you brood of vipers—repent!—an axe, a winnowing fork—the chaff burned with unquenchable fire—repent!

And so, here he is again, John the Baptist, that fierce old Knight of the Woeful Countenance, grim old Puritan, and everybody's least favorite Dutch Uncle. Coming to prepare us for something we are not sure we want to be prepared for. *Preparation D for Doom*, if you please. We thought that we had outgrown him, that he had somehow been dispensed with in form criticism or the doctrine of progressive revelation. But, here he is again, and here we are feeling perhaps strange in his company, and uncomfortable, not so much because we are afraid as because we are somehow disenchanted. The mask that got left over from Halloween doesn't scare us as much as it provides a sense of intrusion. Here we are waiting for the Christmas Parade to begin, and who shows up on the very first float but a sort of Jewish version of Ebeneezer Scrooge!

His camel's hair coat with part of the camel's hide still attached, with the remnants of locusts and wild honey dried in his bushy, tousled beard, with weeks in the wilderness unwashed, we can all but sniff his coming before he arrives, before we can see him, but not before we hear his bugle blast of warning: "REPENT! For the kingdom of heaven is at hand!" Bow-legged and bent from the heat of the searing desert sun, gnarled and wild-eyed from staring at the stars in the cold desert nights.

["You, sir, would you mind moving over and making room for him? Thank you."

"Now, what is it, John the Baptist, you wish to say?"

"REPENT!!!"

"You don't have to say it so loudly. I will tell them. Goodbye. Thanks for dropping in. We will see you next week, perhaps, certainly sometime during the holidays."]

You see, we really will. We always do. There's not enough holly in the world to hide him. There's not enough "Jolly Old St. Nicholas" in the world to drown him out. There's not even enough incense or the smell of plum pudding to quite remove the vaguely disturbing odor.

The truth is, my beloved people, he didn't come from the outside, any more than he just left. He is a part of the Truth that comes from deep within each of us. He is that part of the Good News that first sounds like bad news before it can become Good News.

And the bad part of the Good News is that there really is something for us to do. No matter how He has taken the initiative, no matter how He has emptied Himself and become one of us, and one with us, and one for us, we must, nonetheless, see the wonder of that. Feel the wonder of it deep down within ourselves, from that deep down place where John the Baptist always comes . . . and to where he leads us. We must repent; we must turn from feverish and non-believing ways to the way of surrender and acceptance and belief. We must risk making fools of ourselves in order to know true wisdom; we must turn around in the road and ask what road it is that we are on, and what direction we are taking, and whether that direction takes us ever closer to Him, or ever further away in our own mistaken sense of adequacy. I remember that wonderfully funny and telling line that one of you gave me about your suffering from a *great delusion of adequacy.*

If John the Baptist said nothing else, if he bellowed until he was blue in the face, about nothing else, he told us this, and he keeps on telling us, that until we recognize *the empty place in our hearts where God wants to be*, we are like so many Christmas inns—packed full and busy but devoid of anything that could save us all from the cold, having no room for anything that might save us and make us free.

When I think of John the Baptist, and his unlikely, doleful appearance on the scene, I think of Thomas Hardy, my favorite of all English writers, and of his wonderful little poem called "The Darkling Thrush." In his own time, Hardy found little cause for believing much in mankind or in God either, for that matter. And yet, and yet in all of the gloom of nineteenth-century Wessex, he could write:

"The Darkling Thrush"

I leaned upon a coppice gate
When frost was specter-gray,
And winter's dregs made desolate
The weakening eye of day.

The tangled bine-stems scored the sky
Like strings from broken lyres,
And all mankind that haunted nigh
Had sought their household fires.

The land's sharp features seemed to be
The century's corpse outleant;
His crypt the cloudy canopy,
The wind his death-lament.

The ancient pulse of germ and birth.
Was shrunken hard and dry,
And every spirit upon earth
Seemed fervorless as I.

At once a voice burst forth among
The bleak twigs overhead
In a full-hearted evensong
Of joy illuminated;

An aged thrush, frail, gaunt and small,
In blast-beruffled plume,
Had chosen thus to fling his soul
Upon the growing gloom.

So little cause for carolings
Of such ecstatic sound
Was written on terrestrial things
Afar or nigh around,

That I could think there trembled through
His happy good-night air
Some blessed hope, whereof he knew
And I was unaware.

What an image! That crusty old bird with its feathers askew in the chill wind, in blast-beruffled plume, a darkling thrush indeed . . . but hidden in its heart a hope, and in its song a message of new life to come. It is a wonderful symbol for John the Baptist and for Advent.

Advent. The time just before the adventure begins, When everybody is leaning forward to hear what will happen, even though they know already what will happen and what will not happen, when they listen hard for meaning . . . for *their* meaning, and begin to hear, only faintly at first, the beating of unseen wings.

Is it a plane? Is it a bird? No! It's Super-Jew!! John the Baptizer.

John the Baptist II

What an interesting juxtaposition of titles and names in this Advent reading. Tiberius Caesar, that sullen paranoid, "when he reigned over all of Rome." And then there were all those other lovelies, Pontius Pilate and Caiaphas the High Priest. It would be almost like saying, in a more modern time, "When Adolph Hitler was the Fuhrer of the Third Reich and Franklin D. Roosevelt was the President of the United States and Walter George was the Senator from the state of Georgia, a man named Bubba, the son of Cecil, whose daddy drove a bread truck in Eufala, Alabama, had a real serious case of God and started holding tent meetings along the banks of the Chattahoochee River."

Strange mix. Strange news coming from a strange people in the heart of a strange and melancholy land.

I don't know how it is with you, but Advent is always a kind of melancholy time for me. When I was a little bitty dude, I used to be so revved waiting for Christmas, that's all I could think about. My daddy told me that the days were getting shorter as we approached, and I thought that was wonderful news—that God somehow in his mercy had made the days shorter so that Christmas could get here a lot sooner!

That's not quite the way it works, is it? Even now, we have about thirteen and a half hours of darkness, and that will accelerate until December the 21st. Advent is not simply a season of the church year; it's a season of the flesh, and the church fathers who lived much closer to the earth than you and I felt the melancholy of long nights. The ancients believed that the sun moved away from the earth toward the end of December, and there was always the fear that it would not come back. So they had a celebration called Saturnalia when, at last, the sun seemed to be halted in its movement away from the earth and was gradually coming closer and closer again. It's a melancholy time for us ancients.

It's a stressful time for every one of us—the dread of gift-giving. Is it the right size? Is it the right color? Will she hate it? Or has she already become attached to the ironing board I gave her *last* Christmas? There's a stress in that, especially if you have to go hunting for a parking place, the malls and all the tension that goes with what is really a very simple thing: a baby being born.

What do we make of this John the Baptizer, this melancholy man? In the past, I think I've done him a great disservice. I've spoken of him as *my mother in drag*, the punishing, frightening sounds that bid us change our ways. I don't think so. I think he was a very gentle man. He came to pronounce a baptism, which means a down-pouring, which means a gift from God, a baptism of repentance which doesn't mean feeling rotten about your sins; it means, "Look this way. Look at the one who loves you. Look at the one who forgives you. Look at that." That's the story of your life. And it's a gift from God.

The other day I called my friend John Porter, asking him one more time what we were to make of this man. And he started telling me a tale or two, and then I remembered a tale about him. I think I've told it to one or two of you. One Saturday of every month, John drives a van of parents and wives down to the Macon County Jail where they visit their sons and their husbands who are imprisoned in there. It's a wonderful thing he does. A couple of winters ago, he drove a young woman named Sheena down there to see her husband. Unfortunately, Sheena had on a pair of shorts that did not quite meet the specifications of length that one could wear into the prison, and she was stopped by the guard and told that she could not go in. John was greatly troubled by this; he saw her crying. She was just shattered. And suddenly he had a great idea. He said, "Sheena, you come get in the back of the van." And he started taking off his pants! Now John was a whole lot bigger around than Sheena was, and his legs were a good bit longer. But he handed her the pants, and she put them on. And he said, "One of the tenderest things I've ever seen was seeing her hipping and hopping along to get to the gate where they did, indeed, have to let her in." And I thought that was a kind of John the Baptist sort of thing to do and to be, something kind of crazy to do for the love of God.

I used to think that Advent was sort of the prelude to the joy of Christmas; I now think that Christmas is sort of the post-lude to the melancholy of Advent. And it's the post-lude to everything melancholy in your life and in mine.

For unto us a child is born. Unto us a son is given.

"They all were looking for a king to raise their banners high / Thou camst a tiny baby thing that made a woman cry."

Yeah. Survive Advent if you can. And praise the God who gives us gifts of wonder.

* I add here a poem of Jim's that speaks to this melancholy, a poem he wrote after Midnight Mass one Christmas. I can't be sure that he ever read this poem in a sermon, but it says much as a kind of postscript to this sermon.

"Journey"

With all the candles snuffed,
The sermon said, and
The holy remainder of Bread and Wine
Stored in their holy place;
The altar guild and choir dismissed and thanked
For how lovely it all was,
And every "Merry Christmas" said
And every light turned out,
And door locked on the now dark
Silence of where we – the So Many in our
World of Too Much –
Had once more sought him,
I am the last to leave,
To find my tired way
Through the winter dark of
What is now Christmas Morning,
Across the black, wet streets
And motorway that wend

Toward home and needed rest
And where, like the place I've left,
Everything is comfortable
And much more than enough.

The sky has cleared.
Stars shine above the bleak landscape
Of barren fields that roll toward
The shelter of darkened woods
And a deep silence.
For a moment, a great longing is at once
Revealed and answered
In all that is lean, and sparse, and empty,
And where, in such wilderness,
Lies a promise of unassailable truth.

John the Baptist III

Those words to me, those last words, are among the funniest in all of the Gospels. John the Baptizer is talking about the One who would come with his winnowing fork, burning all the trash and throwing it into the unquenchable fire. And then, says Luke, "And with other such exhortations, he preached to them the good news." *The good news?*

Well, maybe so. John speaks of the ax that has already been laid at the roots of the trees and that every tree that does not bear good fruit should be cut down and burned. What roots? What trees? I think it was a powerful way of his saying that everything you rely on for salvation that is *not God* is nothing more than refuse. So that's good news. The idols turn out to be just exactly that, idols, and all the idolatries that go along with them, just exactly that, idolatries. They had no power to save. And the sooner we come to understand that, maybe the better off we are, the more empowered we are to hear what is the really good news—that we are not all that stuff, that we are more than that stuff; we are more than the things we look upon as investing us with some kind of power that has no God in it. Whatever else repentance meant to John the Baptist, it certainly included taking a hard look at one's self and dealing with the reality of what you see. It was sort of disillusioning, and that's always a gift, you know—to be shorn and shrift of your illusions. Good.

I remember quite a number of years ago, when we had a deacon in this parish, and I, being the supervising priest of that deacon, had to meet once a month with all the other freshly ordained deacons in the diocese to review the progress of their ministries. I remember particularly one young deacon who confessed to us the great sorrow in her heart. She had discovered that the priests and the bishops she had always held high on a pedestal had somehow come down. She didn't tell us what had burst her little balloon or just who it was, but she did let us know that she had discovered that the priests she sort of revered, and one of the bishops, had somehow let her down by being a corrupt, sinful, needy human being just like the rest of us.

Well, what blew me away was the great attention she got from everyone in the group, all hanging on her every tearful word, and trying to coax and commiserate her out of her Slough of Despond so that she might come out and forgive us all and forgive the world for being what the world is. Everyone was really careful about that. Except me. And when all the commiserating was done, I was bold enough to say, "Young woman, this ought to be a time of great rejoicing. You are now rid of your illusions. Welcome to the National Football League. Welcome to the bumps and bruises of finding out the world is sometimes a wicked, corrupt, and needy place and that the people in it, including the clergy, maybe most of all the clergy, are corrupt and sinful and needy people, and maybe the sooner you get it in touch with that, you more will begin to understand the power of the God who loves us just that way and that is dying to save us. Not that ephemeral fairy tale world that you would pull out of a hat, but the world of sinful men and women like you and like me."

Yeah, I kind of think that's what John the Baptist had in mind. Just let's get straight and understand what kind of *in-breaking* love it is that comes to redeem us.

Man, I loved it this morning. I don't mean to embarrass anyone, but I got a whole bunch of telephone calls this morning. They were legitimate, reasonable calls, but the first few were just wonderful. The first question was, "Do we have power at the church?" "Well," I said, and God forgive me, I said, "Well, we have power at the Gable House. I haven't been over to the church yet, but I'm pretty sure we do." What I really wanted to say was, "Yeah, man, we got power. We got power, power in the blood of one who dies for us and lives again so that in our death we may live again." That power. That's all we need and a hell of a lot more than we deserve. Yeah. And may we hang on to it. No, may we let it hang on to us for all the days ahead.

I do need to tell you that this is a Blue Light Special. You get double points for being here this morning. So just take that home with you and put it under the tree for whatever that might mean. But there's something I'd just sort of like to kind of toss out to you if you can stomach this. Suppose you get home this morning or noon, and suppose then that the temperature takes a big dive and the whole country freezes over and stays that way through Christmas afternoon. Suppose you just get stuck in your house, with enough food we would hope, or enough neighbors with four-wheelers who could go and make sure that everyone in the neighborhood had food, but suppose that was about the highest expectation. And then the rest of it would simply be what's gonna happen in your house—

what's gonna happen between you and the people who love you, the people you would give gifts to but you have no gift to give but yourself. Think about that. And if you can make a Merry Christmas out of that, God bless you. And if you can't, God help you. And God help me.

It was the same John the Baptist who not long afterward would see a man coming toward him, a man with Galilean eyes, and he would look deep into face, and then he would say the most beautiful words ever spoken, "Behold, the Lamb of God who takes away the sin of the world."

There is an old Robert Frost Poem I like—it's sort of a winter poem—that is called "Bereft." If you can imagine an old shanty of a farmhouse falling into great disrepair that was once your home or the home of your forebears, Robert Frost goes back to that home, and he says,

> Out on the porch's sagging floor,
> Leaves got up out of a coil and hissed,
> Blindly struck at my knees and missed.
> Something sinister in the tone
> Told me my secret must be known:
> Word I was in the house alone
> Somehow must have gotten abroad,
> Word I was in my life alone,
> Word I had no one left but God.

That's all we need, my dears, because there *is* power, and wonder-working power, in the Lamb of God who takes away the sin of the world.

The Shepherd Knows the Sheep by Name
(Mother's Day)

I've often mentioned my notorious Uncle Henry, the one who taught me every unwholesome bit of information I had about the world. He was a very poor farmer, but he had an eye for business. I've also mentioned to you that the closest I ever came to having a grandparent was my mother's stepmother whom we knew as Mama Jesse. Mama Jesse had married my mother's father late in life, and he had promptly died just a few months afterward. So there was very little of any sort of dynamic relationship between her and any of my grandfather's children. But in good Southern style, there were respects to be paid.

These respects took the form of frequent little trips down to Crawford where we'd go and sit on my Mama Jesse's front porch and sniff the oleander and eat the gummy little cakes that she had prepared for such occasions and talk about everybody's liver. And lungs. And heart. And gallbladder. I came to think of these occasions as organ recitals of a sort! And they were dismal and dreadful recitals, and as soon as we could do so, we would all leave. And I suspect that Mama Jesse was more glad to see us gone than we were glad to be gone.

One of the things I respected about Uncle Henry— one of the few things you could respect about Uncle Henry—was that he never attended these little soirees. He had his own little thing going with Mama Jesse. As I said, he had an eye for business, and Mama Jesse had somehow become bequeathed with a modest financial income, and every time there was a need to make a small loan (and because he was a poor farmer, there were often those occasions), he would pick up his old dilapidated buggy (my Uncle Henry never got an automobile in this life, and I doubt if he got one in the life beyond), he would hitch up his dilapidated buggy to his dilapidated horse, and we would ride seven miles up the dirt road. He let me go on these occasions, and I played the role of the carriage attendant. He even bought me a cap for it. We would go over, and we would pick up Mama Jesse, and my job was to fluff up the cushions and help him hoist the old girl up in the back seat, and we would ride through Crawford, and she would nod like Queen Victoria and wave her little hankie, like royalty, to all her friends. Uncle Henry sat there, beaming like a Cheshire cat, savoring the benefits, and even with what little innocence I still had then, I sort of sensed that Mama Jesse was being taken for a ride in more ways than one! And what I loved about the old girl is that I sensed that she knew that, too. She was nobody's fool. She was simply playing the game because she enjoyed the game, and if it gave my Uncle Henry some sense of earning his bounty, then so much the better.

Well, in the context of that homely little recollection, I'd like to wish all of you a Happy Mother's Day. I heard just the other day, a woman of some considerable intelligence share an opinion with which I have profound sympathy. She was a woman obviously engaged in the corporate business structure, and she was talking about women, and she said, "Men have company annuities, expense accounts, profit-sharing plans, and country club privileges. We have Mother's Day." And I suspect that if any of you mothers who is sensitive to that issue were to give credence to what is going on today, you might have the slightest sense that you're once more being taken for a ride. It won't be the first time, and it probably won't be the last. But it does raise very legitimate questions about what it is in the gospel that really honors the people we care about and makes a healthy response to the authorities in the world that nurture us and without whom we would be deprived of the infinite possibilities of our own lives. I would like to think, dear women, that we would not have this sacred space take you for any kind of a ride and that we would remember you for the precious person you are and, in light of that, bless you for the relationship you have with us.

And what more appropriate thing to be thinking about than shepherding. Shepherding and mothering are much alike, when you do them right. Now it's interesting to remember that this little lesson that he gave the disciples came immediately after that healing of the blind man in John's Gospel about three or four Sundays ago. Jesus had healed this man who was born blind, and the Pharisees heard about it, and they heard also that he healed him on the Sabbath. And they weren't too thrilled about that because they had their precious little formula which did not include healing on the Sabbath. It was against the laws of Judaism. So in good Simon and Garfunkel fashion, they went to this man who had been healed and said, "'We'd like to know a little bit about you for our files. We'd like to help you learn to help yourself.' So tell us what you know of this Jesus, who allegedly heals alleged blindness." And that wonderful man said, "Well, you know, the truth is I've been so busy looking and seeing God's beautiful world that I haven't given a lot of thought to it, but my imagination would tell me that he must come from God." And the Pharisees didn't care too much for that, either, so they cast him out of the community. And when Jesus heard about it, he was peeved, not just a little bit, and he too went and sought that man and said, "Do you truly believe that I who healed you am the son of God?" And he said, "If you say so."

It is *then* that he turned to his disciples and said, "Whoever comes in by any way other than the sheep gate is a robber and thief." And the sheep know the voice of the shepherd. And the shepherd knows the sheep by name. Isn't that interesting? And they really do. This was quite the literal parable. Did you know that even to this day in Palestine and in Greece, the shepherds name their sheep and call them by name the same way you would call your dog or cat or your child? The shepherd knows their names; he knows them by that alone, not by their number, not by their color, their circumstance, not by anything else that would diminish their true and precious value. That's what the shepherd knows.

And what does the sheep know about the shepherd? Well, among other things, they know him when he comes in the right door. In those days, you know, shepherds and sheepfolds and those kinds of things were for that economy what the bank vault is to ours. It contained everything that was valuable, all of their livelihood and wealth. And the sheep door was not a lovely little thing; it was a heavy iron door just like the door to the bank vault. And it was called the thorough; it gives us the root to modern words like "thoroughfare." The man who guided it was called the thoroughroast. And he had an awful responsibility. Only the shepherd was allowed in this heavy door. Even the owner of the sheep could not go in without this shepherd. Jesus says, in a strange metaphor, "I am the door, and I am the shepherd, and the sheep know me when I call them by their names. And they know my voice." And believe it or not, that's scientifically true, too. A Bible commentator tells the story of the Scotsman who went to Palestine, thinking he had a theory about why the sheep follow the shepherd. He thought it had to do with the shepherd's clothing and the smell that was on them. I guess, the smell you get being a shepherd has a distinctive flavor all its own. And so he challenged one of the Palestinian shepherds to swap clothes, and he did. The sheep still followed the shepherd dressed in all Scottish attire. They recognized his voice. And what does his voice say? The fascinating thing is it's not always so important what that voice says; it's how that voice *says it* and *if it takes you for a ride.*

He comes, as we said last Sunday, softly to the door and knocks and waits for you to ask him in. He doesn't yell, he doesn't command, he doesn't give orders as much as he asks us to enter into conversation with him.

I don't know how you feel about it, but when I was in the fifth grade, they told me when I was in the sixth grade, I could boss people around. When I was in the seventh grade, they told me when I was in the ninth grade, I could boss people around. When I was a senior in high school, they told that when I went off to college, I could boss people around. Then, they told me when I started work, I could boss people around. Man, did that sound good to me. I don't know how that sounded to you, but it sounded pretty good to me.

The funny thing is, the sad thing is, I think that sometimes that does sound good to you. Do you know when I hear the best comments about my sermon is when I really rev it up, lay it down, and maybe sound like a boss. And people say, "You were really on target today, Father Callahan." Maybe so. And maybe I spoke of the shepherd's word, but I did not speak with the shepherd's voice. Anything that puts you down is of the kingdom of darkness. And people who would fight the kingdom of darkness by ascribing some tyranny to our Lord do a wicked and blind and foolish thing. He coaxes us, he loves us, he leads us, and we know, above everything else in the world, he cares about us. That's what shepherds do. They care about the sheep; they lay down their lives for them. And whenever we bring indignation and pettiness and hate and anger into the world, we make the work of the shepherd all that harder.

What do I know about Mother's Day? Whatever I know, oddly enough, I've learned from my children. Once I had an experience that was so moving to me I wrote a poem. I don't do this to you often, but I'm going to read you this poem which comes out of my little book of poems (on sale at Monk's Chevron Filling Station and Grocery, 15 cents a copy!). After this experience, this is what I wrote.

The Givenness of Things

TO MY SON JOHN

The sound of your name, John,
is more miracle to me
than metaphor of oak or leaf
could bear.
No tree could reach for sun
and make such shape as you,
Nor could one run!

More like a god you are to me
and fair, dear God, how fair!

When on the beach you ran
and when the young Sun God
shed tears, I swear
the earth stood still;
and never did a penitent
so grieve offending God
as I of wounding thee.

What shall I do, the father
of such laughing, loving
God as you,
To learn it is a god who seeks
to please the godless me?

I'll make amends . . .
give you back your tears
and love you, love you,
my son John,
through all these loveless years.

If you don't understand it, and rather mediocre poetry is rarely understood, then like our dear Lord did with parables, I will explain the parable to you.

It was after a long cold winter, and I'd been on the road a good, long time. I was just starting a new enterprise, and we didn't have much money. The good fortune was, and some of you will understand this, the credit card companies didn't know that yet. So summertime came, and I was at home at last, and we could go on vacation. We took the credit card with us to that wonderful middle class mecca, Panama City Beach. We rented an affordable room in a very exquisite hotel, and everything I could rent with that credit card, I rented. I rented a super-speed surfboard. I'd never been on a surfboard in my life, much less a super-speed one. And I gathered up the surfboard, and I gathered up John Callahan who was seven and a half years old. That was "B. B." before braces. He had a little mouthful of crooked teeth and a great little towhead, and he and I were alive with confidence and excitement, his warranted, mine not! We got into the surf, and I started showing him how it was to be done. After about fifteen aborted attempts, I was black and blue from trying to stay on this surfboard, I had swallowed more surf than I had surfed on, and finally in an exhausted gesture, I turned to John and said, "Would you like to try?" We pushed the surfboard out to where it was way over his head but not over mine. I put John up on it, stationed him right in the middle of the board, and he stood there, and I gently nudged the surfboard, and it rode the crest of the wave in the first time absolutely perfect as was every other time after that. Like a little Sun God, he went sailing in. And every time, I had to go in and pick that bloody surfboard up, because it was as heavy as he was, he couldn't manage it, and he kept doing it over and over again. And you know, something really sick and sad, something childish and churlish took over in me. As I look back, I suspect it was because he could do it and I couldn't, because I wanted to show off for *him*, and here he was showing off for me. So after about thirty of these trips, I said, "Well, if you're big enough to enjoy the surf, you're big enough to carry out the surfboard." And I turned my back on him, and I walked out toward the beach. After awhile I turned around, and there he was, not in the surf at all, sitting on the beach with his head down between his knees. He was crying his heart out. I had ruined what had been a wondrous and joyous and happy time. And I felt miserable. And I went to him and picked him up, and I said, "Son, please, will you ever, ever be able to forgive me for what I just did?" He was so full of tears at this point that he couldn't speak. He was just all tied up in knots, but he nodded, "Uh-hmm." I said, "Can you *really* forgive me?" "Uh-hmm." And all of a sudden, he was the father, and I was the son. He forgave me, and I felt that I could go on living. And the miracle of that I don't know for sure, but I suspect the miracle of that kind of forgiveness, that kind of relationship between human beings, as that blind man recognized, comes only from God.

You remember when our Lord was at the Last Supper, according to Mark's recollection, after they had finished the meal and were about to leave, he said, "You know, those who pretend to be rulers of the Gentiles lord it over them, and their mighty men exercise hard authority over them. But it shall not be so among you. Whoever would be first, let him be your servant. Whoever would be the greatest of all, let him be the slave of all. Whoever would love you as a shepherd loves you, let him be your mother."

Happy Mother's Day.

Feeding the Multitude

"Now when Jesus heard this . . . he withdrew in a boat to a lonely place apart."

When Jesus heard *what?*

Funny how the lectionary skips around. Last week we finished up with chapter 13 of Matthew's gospel and the lovely parables of the kingdom: the mustard seed, the treasure in the field, the pearl of great price, the big fat net full of fishes, God's big fat heart full of us. All that good stuff.

Today we come to more good stuff—about the feeding of the five thousand, about the parish life commission setting up for a great picnic, only they forgot to form a good committee—about five thousand hungry Hebrews, not counting women and children, because in Matthew's day they didn't count, so make it ten thousand all tolled, with about half of them wanting Happy Meals! And there stand the disciples and *Murray,*[2] looking nothing at all like Ronald McDonald, looking rather a bit bewildered, impatient not just with the crowd but with Jesus too, who had let the whole day slip by without much thought to details like *supper* and night time at a lonely, isolated place.

Of course, we know how it all ends—how with just a couple of catfish and five loaves of day-old bread, Jesus sprung for a banquet that would make Julia Child's look like a piker.

---

[2] Jim created a fictional thirteenth disciple named Murray, very Jewish, and used him in many sermons.

John sentimentalizes the story and says that it was a "young lad" who volunteered his lunch—or had it jerked from him by Simon Peter! The other three gospel writers suggest that the loaves and catfish came from one of the disciples, Murray no doubt, the same lunch he forgot to pack when they got caught plucking grain on the Sabbath. Anyway, those were the fixings, and oddly enough, there is no account by any of the four gospel-writers of a direct mention of there being a miracle: no hocus-pocus, no shazam. *Just Jesus taking the bread and the fish and giving thanks and passing it around.* That's the way most miracles go, isn't it? We hardly notice them. Somehow, the evangelists took note of that fact. Almost playfully, they let us know that something incredible took place without going into detail. They let us know, for instance, that there was enough left over from the two fish and five loaves to feed everybody in the precinct, including the Baptists . . . and there were probably lots of them even then! Indeed, a little known fact is that this was the occasion for the invention of the "doggy bag."

So, we know how it all ends. What we don't know, or what we have forgotten if we did, is how it all *begins*. And how it begins has a great deal to do with the wonder of what happened and how it ends and what is forever happening and how it is forever ending.

"Now when Jesus heard this . . ." Heard what? And that sends us back to the part that the church fathers, in their infinite wisdom, decided to skip so we could get on to the good stuff. And when you go back and read it, you can

readily understand why they decided to skip over it. It is the gory little episode of the beheading of John the Baptist. Just a minor little detail. Like telling the story of the Civil War days and leaving out the assassination of Abraham Lincoln. Or telling about Little Red Riding Hood and leaving out the wolf.

The martyrdom of John the Baptist is central to the gospel story. The seamy account of Herod's little banquet and all the grotesque particulars of Salome's swirling dance and her mother's vicious fury and the serving up of the Baptist's severed head on a platter (only Matthew gives us these details) are full of dramatic import. The event is a devastating blow to our Lord and has its shattering impact at all points of his vulnerability. His love for the man who signaled his coming, who baptized him in the River Jordan—that would have been enough. But far more than that, John the Baptist was the bellwether, the very symbol, of the hope of Israel. He pointed like a great search light beyond the misery and oppression of the poor, the people, the dispossessed, and the hopeless. It was out of his ministry of hope and promise that our Lord himself emerged, and for all that differentiated their separate paths, John was dearer to him and to his mission than any person on earth! Moreover, he knew that what happened to John, or something worse, would sooner or later happen to him. Indeed, already Herod regarded him and his mighty works as evidence of John the Baptist risen from the dead, which in Herod's lethal logic meant that they would have to make him dead again!

We can only try to imagine the meaning of all of this to Jesus and to the twelve. But at least we can understand why he would, after hearing this dreadful news, seek out a quiet, a hidden, and a lonely place and, for a moment at least, draw apart from the wretchedness, the sadness, the cruelty of Herod's rotten and punishing world.

The Feeding of the Five Thousand

A former student of mine once gave me a little book of cartoons, the title of which I forget. It's a harmless and good-humored bit of irreverence about the disciples, mostly, made up of delightful little stick-figures and simple faces which poke fun at nothing sacred but which suggest rightly that the disciples were probably as human we are, if not more so. One of my favorites is the Last Supper. They are all seated at the table, and one of the guileless ones is beaming with excitement and anticipation as he tells his neighbor, "I just love it when we eat out!"

There's another that's just as funny to me. The topic is that of our Gospel lesson today—the feeding of the five thousand.

Jesus stands there firm and poised with satisfaction at the mound of bread and fishes his prayer has just produced, and there is the inevitable bolt of lightning still hanging suspended in the cartoon manner of things, just above the pile of food. One of the disciples, probably Thomas, is saying in an aside to his fellow disciples, "He forgot the tartar sauce." Any way you look at it, it's funny, funny because it is irreverent and because it adds a bit of upbeat modernity to what usually rests in our minds as archaic and beyond apprehension, certainly beyond our grasp.

We've never known quite what to do with miracles. Not because they don't ever happen, but, to the contrary, because they've become so *commonplace*. Because it's so much easier to enlarge on what's *missing* in our lives than to give thanks and to live gratefully for what's been given us. Someone told me about the exploit of a couple of bored college students who were working the summer at Old Faithful Inn at Yellowstone. The legendary geyser is just a couple of hundred yards from the Inn, and several rows of benches line the area where the tourists sit and wait for the geyser to erupt. The two students took their place a modest distance apart but within view of the tourists. They had an old steering wheel off an automobile attached to some pipe they had found somewhere, and while the rapt tourists watched Old Faithful steam hundreds of feet up into the air, just as it began to dissipate, one student yelled to the other, "Okay, Clyde! Shut her down." What made the event even funnier was that most of the husbands walked off saying something like, "I told you, Wanda Sue, that they did it with the plumbing!"

Even the wonders of Nature and the mysteries that fill our lives we feel better about believing that the government controls, that a summer student turns on or off, that it's done with mirrors or with the plumbing. And even those explanations turn out to be unsatisfactory; in any crowd of disciples, there will always be someone to remind us, "He forgot the tartar sauce." Not all men worship God, indeed, but sooner or later all of us—those who worship him included—find it quite convenient to be his critics! And if we have problems about miracles, generally they stem from the fact that he hasn't done the ones we want him to. Or that the ones he *has* done don't quite measure up to our expectations. Not *medium rare*. So we send it back.

According to Matthew, he did this one, without even being asked. Jesus had gone out to pray and to be alone, to get away from it all for awhile. The people in town heard that he was about and went flocking to where they found him. He gave up his own plans for refreshment and stayed there with them, "and healed their sick," says Matthew. Then the disciples came to him as the day drew to an end and reminded Jesus that it was a lonely place, that it had been a long day, and that the people should be sent home to their towns and villages to get something to eat. "Give them something to eat yourselves," Jesus said, and they told him that they only had five loaves and a couple of fish. Then he asked that the food be brought to him. Then he said the blessing, and what a blessing it was. By the time they had passed it all around, they had fed five thousand, give or take some women and children, says Matthew, and there was enough left over to fill up twelve baskets—maybe a not so complimentary reference to the twelve basket-heads who called themselves disciples.

To understand the message that St. Matthew sends us is not only to accept the miracle, but, more importantly, the meaning of the miracle. It portends so much . . . so much about suppers and about Last Suppers, so much about bread and about Jesus being the Bread of Life. Indeed, the fare was simple and plain. Bread and fish. Because Jesus knew the people were simply hungry, and to men who were simply hungry, he simply fed them. And there was much left over. As there always is.

And what does this have to say to the hungry and lonely and frightened men who first heard it in the first century church? And what does it have to say to us, the over-fed, overly-indulged, miracle-weary, would-be disciples of a later day? A much, much later day? The same thing it said then. That God is *bread*, that He is life itself, that he is the simplicity of our survival and the staff of our very existence. That to try to live apart from him and from his laws of love and repentance and forgiveness and reconciliation is to the soul and to the spirit what living apart from bread, water, and meat are to the body. That he gives himself generously and with abandon, like some crazy sower who throws seeds everywhere, like some crazy father who forgives his Prodigal Son everything under the sun just for the joy of having him home again. Home again where he belongs! Home again where you and I belong too, because it's where happiness is, and you and I were made for happiness—not suffering and sadness and forsakenness but joy and peace and home! That's what we were made for.

Our chief problem, or at least *my* chief problem, is not so much that I don't believe that he makes bread . . . that his is bread, and wine, but that I have a tendency to refuse the bread that he gives me. My life is full of it, as is yours. And the saddest commentary on the sordid little story of my life is not what I haven't gotten at his hands but the uneaten meals, the shunned invitations, the banquets ignored, with not only fish and bread and wine but tartar sauce and plum pudding to boot!

One reason we have lying around for mistrusting miracles is that it keeps life uncluttered. It keeps us from facing the prospect of encountering God on any terms but our *own*! It has not always been thus with me, and I hope to God that it is no longer thus with me. I remember a time, a time that my present working situation constantly reminds me of these days. As you know, I spend most of my week days in Charlotte, North Carolina. About twenty years ago I was spending time there then, too. Of all things, I was selling *fish*—working for a zany old crony of mine who gave me a job because he couldn't stand to see a grown man cry; moreover, he couldn't even bear to see a grown man frown, so he made me a vice-president in his company, Trans Marine Seafood we were. We were going broke faster than our wares were thawing, and about two thirds of the reasons were *me,* and I knew it. I had left the ministry for this. For food that I couldn't sell, in places that I couldn't fathom, and in a sense of aloneness that was fifty fathoms deep and darker than doom.

I was sitting one morning in the restaurant of a rather crummy motel, as I recall—"The Heart of Charlotte"— which is itself a bit ironic because I wasn't aware that Charlotte had one. *I was not even sure that I did.* I had no heart for this or for the sense of forsakenness that I felt at the time. I was sitting there dawdling over my coffee with my hands in my lap, indeed, with my life in my lap. Two priests came in for coffee. One was a tall stately man, who turned out to be the Abbot of Belmont Abbey. The other was just a fat little priest with a cherubic face. They looked like an ecclesiastical version of Laurel and Hardy, and after a few minutes of observing me, it was Hardy, the one with the fat cherubic face, who asked if they could join me. I remembered a cute line from college days and said that they were welcomed but that I didn't realize I was becoming unjoined! They didn't laugh. Because they knew and I knew that I *was*. They couldn't have been any more gentle. They couldn't have been more perceptive or sensitive to the apparent lostness of a fellow pilgrim. They couldn't have been more God-sent. You might tell me that it was by blind chance that they happened in for coffee at a place where I just happened to be, and I would have to tell you that you were right. And you might tell me that I was simply lucky, and again I would tell you that you were right. And then when we got through all of this sane and sensible conversation and you asked me who sent them, I would tell you *God*. God sent them. Jesus sent them. They were incarnate Jesuses in the same way you and I are when he sends us into the midst of blind chance and dumb luck, into the random and witless events of our own days and everybody else's. And if you asked me why he doesn't send somebody or himself into some of the tragedy and pathos of the miserable life of so much of mankind, I would answer that I simply do not know, because I am not God, but that it would be my guess that he does send someone, himself included, but that we are too busy trying to be gods ourselves to notice or to hear or to receive, too glutted with our own importance to hunger for the food that he lays before us.

I hungered that day. Before the coffee had gotten cold, I told those two men of God how empty and aching and alone I was and how I didn't see much point in going on. I barely remember anything they said. But I remember what they did. They invited me out to Belmont Abbey, where the tall one was the Abbot and where the short fat one had to teach a class at two o'clock. We had lunch with some of the students, a boisterous lot, but good company, and I was introduced as an important visitor just passing through. I was invited to sit in on the class, and as I best recall it was a class in seventeenth century English literature, and it dealt with the poetry of John Donne, and it included a line that has stayed with me for twenty years, "Difference of sex no more we knew / Than our Guardian Angells doe." I don't remember just what it was I listening to, whether it was the stammering intensity of Donne, or the warmth and glow of that ebullient little priest who took such delight in it as he read. I suppose really that it was the stammering intensity of the goodness that had been so gratuitously laid before me, laid at my feet, like a prodigal who comes in out of the storm and finds the fire full ablaze and bread and meat on the table and a family that has longed for his coming home.

Thinking about all this sent me back to Belmont Abbey several weeks ago. I pass it on my way home every week. It's just a few miles south of Charlotte, just off I-85. I generally look for its rather grim old twin Gothic towers and the spire of a steeple that reaches high into the air. I turned off the other day and went in and asked if anybody could tell me who the Abbot was in 1961 and if they could tell me if a rather portly gentleman of a priest who taught English literature might still be about. The lady they conducted me to ran the bookstore. She happens to be an Episcopalian. She told me that, of course, she knew who that Abbot was, that he was retired and was on vacation at the time but would be back this fall. As for the portly priest, who else could that be than Father Garrick. I had mentioned to her that he took me to dinner at the Charlotte City Club and gave me my first whiskey sour. She laughed and said that it had to be him because he was the only priest who ever had a membership there. She told me that he had died about five years ago, and for some reason I recalled that that was at about the same time I had begun my new preparation for a priesthood of my own. She asked me if I would care to see his picture, and I said that, of course, I would. She told me to prepare myself, as she opened up a storage room door just a few feet behind her and up a couple of steps. And there it was. A picture bigger than life itself. One of those hugely enlarged pictures like the ones they used to put out in front of movie houses of Clark Gable or Irene Dunn, only this one was Oliver Hardy! Father Garrick himself, beaming as though he had just downed a couple of whiskey sours. It was something they had had around for some kind of reunion, and I almost found myself asking if it were for sale, but I couldn't have gotten it into my car because it was so huge. But it was the man who had saved me from drowning or from simply going under.

It sent me back to John Donne too, back to finally look up the poem from which came those delightful little lines about an innocent love of his. "Difference of sex no more we knew / Than our Guardian Angells doe." Well, it turns out the poem wasn't all that innocent. The name of it is "Relique," and Donne is wishing at the time that some grave digger might one day unearth his bones along with those of his lover and take them to some Bishop as holy relics, and some of it I dare not read, except for this little ending:

First, we loved well and faithfully,
Yet knew not what we loved nor why;
Difference of sex no more we knew,
Than our Guardian Angells doe . . .
These miracles we did; but now alas,
All measure and all language, I should pass,
Should I tell what a miracle was she!

What a miracle was she! What a miracle was John Donne. And what a miracle was Father Garrick. What a miracle we all are, and our lives are filled miraculously with such bread, such sustenance as to startle our best imagination.

I Will Make You Fishers of Men

The place is important. It always is in the Gospels. And sometimes *where* he said it has great importance in our understanding of *what* he said. What he said to Andrew and Peter, to James and John, in calling them to follow him and be his disciples, what he said was, "I will make you fishers of men." And what he meant was colored by where he said it. He said it at Capernaum, a bustling, teeming, commercial market where fishing from the Sea of Galilee was the major industry, and where an international highway brought every kind and color of human being in the known world— among them cut-throats and second story men and hustlers and hookers and horse traders. It was not where you would want to send your daughter to a summer camp, or your son either, unless he carried a gun. Capernaum was Five Points in downtown Atlanta. It was Chicago and Detroit and Pittsburgh, only with the smell of fish and garlic and cheap perfume.

This is where Jesus told these men to follow him. He didn't invite them. He didn't tell them what a wonderful tour he had to offer with stops in all the best hotels and a continental breakfast compliments of the house. No. He didn't ask them if they were keen on a swell adventure and improving themselves and doing something that would make their mothers proud of them. No. He commanded them! It was a friendly enough commandment, genial, yet full of authority: kindly, yet imperial. It gets watered down in the English into "Follow me." In the original Greek, however, it was "Here! After me." It was the same kind of loving command that my mother gives me when I go home now, and we are sitting down to the table, and she says, "Here! Right by me. I want you to sit right by me."

I made a wonderful discovery this week: it's the very same verb he uses later in Matthew, in the eleventh chapter, when he addresses those who labor and are heavy laden. Instead of "Come unto me . . . ," it's "Here! After me. And I will give you rest."

And what did he mean by telling these *sea people* that he would make them fishers of men? Well, figure it out for yourself. It's high time we did. The world is going to hell in a bucket while the church busies itself with liturgical renewal or cheerier hymns! It's time we figured it out for ourselves.

I mis-learned what it meant a long, long time ago. I had just declared for the ministry, and I became the *object d'art*, the curio, if not the victim of every interest group in the First Methodist Church. I was the Boy Wonder who would go out and slay their particular form of dragon or be fed to the lions, or both. I had no training nor much propensity for what they wanted me to do. I had only heard, however vaguely, and however freighted with mystery, the voice of One who had said, "Here! After me." And I had said, "Okay."

One, in particular, I remember and wish I could forget. In the words of Mark Twain, he was a good man in the worst sense of the word. He had made a large fortune as a local merchant and also as a slum lord. He collected burdensome rents from the poor miserable ones who had no option but to live in his pig pens, and he eased his conscience by passing out religious tracts to them, which he got for free from some off-the-wall publishing house. "He's a good Christian man," my mother said, "and you should go with him." If she had only known—the arrogance, the self-righteousness, the contempt he had for everyone who didn't share his narrow views. He didn't drink, or smoke, or curse. He didn't go to the movies. All he did was grind the faces of the poor and talk about how good the Lord had been to him and Hilda. He was Mrs. Grundy in drag. And there I was going around town in his Hudson Hornet as we collected the rents and passed out the tracts and asked people who didn't have enough to eat if they had been saved. The only bright light in all this was one day when he asked a stranger that question, and the old man said, "Yeah, have you?" To which Mr. Grundy replied, "Of course!" And the old man made my day when he said, "Well, you sho' don't look like it." That was as close, I think, as Mr. Grundy ever came to cursing.

I'll tell you what Jesus meant when he said to those sea people, "I will make you fishers of men." It's exactly what the ghost of Jacob Marley meant when a frightened and shaking Ebenezer Scrooge tried to pal up to him: "You were always good at business," he said. And Jacob Marley said, "MANKIND . . . WAS . . . MY . . . BUSINESS." Do you remember? It's your business too, and mine. And it's a messy business. We don't get off the hook by asking people if they've been saved. We get into the thick of it by living lives which have about them a saving quality, and not only in what we say but in what we are: to stand—"Here! After me"—to stand with Christ in his sinful and broken world, to witness to what is sinful and broken in us, to be lonely with those who are alone, and to have an ear for the voice of the poor, and to have a heart for those who are broken hearted, including Mr. Grundy. Perhaps most of all Mr. Grundy.

Mankind is a messy business. And in the midst of that business we are to praise and adore and worship God. And sometimes it's perfectly fine to use those words—to praise him and give him thanks, and to do it openly and without shame. And sometimes we simply need to speak in daily language which men and women can hear and for which they are dying for somebody to say.

Sermon on the Mount at Long John Silver's

One of the many things I love about the Gospel according to Saint Luke is that Luke just doesn't mess around very much; he's so eager to share those wonderful tales, parables of our Lord, so eager to rush to the heart of the matter that he speaks sometimes with a very plain tongue. And his plainness sheds light on some important differences.

This account is of the people who came to hear Jesus after he'd been thrown out of his own hometown, how they thronged about him, touched him, did all they could to be near because power came out of him, and he healed them all, says Saint Luke. And then looking at his disciples and facing this strange multitude who'd come from far and near, the Gentiles from Tyre and Sydon, those wretched people, according to Jewry, and all the others, those honored ones from Jerusalem and throughout all Judea. And then Jesus speaks to them, and Luke is very careful to identify the landscape, in a "level place," he says. In St. Matthew, it's known as the Sermon on the Mount with Jesus standing loftily above the people. For a dramatic landscape, it's lovely to behold, but it's not true to his character, and Luke has him standing eye to eye with the people on level ground.

And he looks them in the eyes, especially his disciples, and he says "Blessed are you"—not "Blessed are *the*" but "Blessed are *you* poor." And he doesn't qualify it with "in spirit." Blessed are *you* poor, for yours is the kingdom of

God. Blessed are you who hunger; you will be satisfied. Blessed are you who weep now, for you shall laugh.

And then that wonderful passage as he looks at those, the rich, the proud, the self-assured who will soon be putting him to death along with his disciples later, he says, "And blessed are you when men exclude you and revile you and mock you." One day you will dance, he says. Well, so far, so good.

But then Woe is Me. Woe to you who are rich—and don't start thinking about the Fortune 500 because everyone of us in this room today, compared to about nine tenths of the world's population, we live like kings and princes. That's the way it goes in our society. Woe to you who are rich.

And then he says the key word, "Woe to you who are full now." What does that mean? In my case, I think it means "Woe to you when you are *full of yourself*." I said last week that most of my sin comes out of fear; when it doesn't come out of fear, it comes out of those moments when I am full of myself. And for a while, that feels so good, but later, sooner, comes the hurting word that stings like a wasp or the pretense that is as phony as a seven dollar bill. And, once again, I am empty.

Joe's not here, so I can tell this story, and if you don't like it, blame it on him. Joe Cumming told me this wonderful story about Mr. Taft. He became the twenty-seventh President of the United States and later Chief Justice. Mr. Howard Taft. One day he was gathered with a group of attorneys, and a brilliant American barrister named Chauncey DePugh was called upon to introduce the great Mr. Taft. He talked for about fifteen or twenty minutes, talking about how someone much worthier than he should have had this honor, but the committee couldn't find one so he was kind of stuck. And he talked about himself a great deal, and then finally he got around to introducing Mr. Taft. And he said, "A man pregnant with the ideas and ideals of democracy who is taking us into a new era, Mr. Taft." Now, if you know anything about Mr. Taft, he was huge of girth. Big giant of a man. And he stood looking over the crowd and at Mr. Chauncey DePugh, and he said, "Pregnant, indeed? If it's a boy, I shall name it George Washington. If it's a girl, I shall name it Martha Washington. But if it's, as I suspect, a large pocket of gas, I shall name it Chauncey DePugh!"

God have mercy on the Chauncey DePugh that is in me. That's one of the curses of the clergy—we become so full of ourselves, and so high-minded, and so forgetful of a Savior who's meek and lowly of heart. And we join hands with the oppressors. I remember that wonderful line from *The Color Purple*, Alice Walker's painfully wonderful book. She has the heroine talking about the oppressor, and she says, "He make you think he be everywhere. And when you begin to think he be everywhere, he be God." The oppressor. Woe to you who are so full of yourselves that you oppress and the leave the rest of us out.

I am glad Luke had him standing on a level place, brother to mankind looking them straight in the eye.

{posturing} This is a silly kind of a posture, isn't it? This is the way the priest stands when he says the prayer of consecration. I used to think, "Man, I wish I didn't have to do that." But I do. And the reason I do, it sounds like something from a textbook; it's called the "Orans" position. And what it says is I am unarmed, I am emptyhanded, I couldn't hurt a fly, we need you, we expect you to come and break bread with us. One thing I love about the Gospel is that every time, almost every time, someone kneels before Jesus, the first thing he tells them is to get up. Stand up. And that great Eucharistic prayer says something about blessing for he has made us worthy to *stand* before him as his poor, as his blessed.

Last Monday night I got caught in a squeeze. I had to speak out at the college on Death and Dying. I'm becoming more of an expert than I choose to be. The class began at 5:30, and the professor was absent, so I had to hold class. At 7:30 I had a vestry meeting, and I needed to get there on time. Peg had a commitment, so I told her I would just squeeze in something to eat, and my heart and soul took me down to Long John Silvers, that noble establishment. I went in for some fish and chips, and I was surprised that about 6:40 in the evening the place was all but empty. I went in and was served almost immediately, and then right behind me, a couple that I recognized but I could not place them to save my life. And then I remembered, they were the man and woman who had played Mr. and Mrs. Fezziwig in *A Christmas Carol,* and there they were with their eight little Fezziwigs. And Mr. Fezziwig allowed as how they had just gotten the last four, so I assume that they were adopted or fostered. They were beautiful and beautifully behaved. Mr. Fezziwig took account of everyone who wanted slaw and those who didn't. Then he counted his money and made his order, and the food was brought to them.

And then into the establishment came a woman, frail and somewhat ravaged. She and her country parents, who were much, much too old to have a daughter her age, but they came in with her, and they sat down at a table, and she had her eye on me. I was thrilled to death until I remembered, of course, that I had on my collar and my blue shirt and my cross. She kept looking at me until I was uncomfortable, and finally she left her booth and came over and sat right by me, and asked, of course, that interesting question, "Are you a priest?" And I said, "Ma'am, who else would be dressed this ridiculously?" And she took it as a rebuff and said, "I'm sorry. I'm interrupting your meal." And I said, "No, no. Forgive me. I was just trying to be funny. Yes, I am a priest." I thought the next question would be, "Why do you wear a blue shirt instead of a black one?" Or "What kind of cross is that?" Or "Do Episcopalians believe in God?" But no. She said, "I would like to ask you to pray for me. I haven't much believed in God of late. My mother and dad are taking me down to Columbus where I'm to check in to the detox center for addiction. And while I haven't had much faith in God lately, I'd like you to pray for me." I said, "Of course, I will. But the important thing, ma'am, is *how much faith he has in you*. That's what matters." And she said, "Really?" And I said, "Oh, yes." And then I asked her her name. Her name was Sandy. She gave me her last name, and I said, "I will pray for you, and so will all my people. You must have a great deal of courage. And God really knows what to do with that. And when it runs out, know that we will be praying for you." She seemed pleased with that, and she went back to the table, and in a rather clear, loud voice rehearsed with her mother and father every word that we had exchanged. And they looked at me for the first time without suspicion. It was very nice.

By this time, my fish and chips had gotten very cold, so I made short work of them, and went over to the Fezziwigs' place where they occupied three booths, thanked them for letting me see those lovely, well-behaved children, asked them if they enjoyed their meal. They said, "Oh yes, it's wonderful." I went up and introduced myself to the mother and father of Sandy. And I said, " I know you must be *proud* of her, how much courage she has." I started to tell them about, you know, some of my favorite lines from *The Wizard of Oz*, "Who put the ape in the apricot, what makes the Hottentot so hot, what do they got that I don't got? Courage." And then I thought better of that.

And I left the place and realized that there just for a moment, Long John Silver's had turned into a kind of chapel for us poor. And I had the strange feeling that I had just received Communion because, of course, I had. I had. And I invite you to that same communion who fills the empty and who loves us all for Christ's sake.

A Galilean Story

Really and truly, it's a story not about fish or about fishing. That's the context because that's the context in which Simon Peter lived and had his living. It's also the context in which Jesus met him that day, which is usually the case. It's not about fish or fishing. It's about grace and wonder and mystery and trust.

The story is a little bit convoluted, according to Luke. Luke is good about leaving out pertinent details so he can get to what is most important to him, namely the revelation of who Jesus is. It's the old Galilean story.

If you grew up, as I did, a Methodist, we were fond of doing what in those days was called a Galilean service where the preacher got in a boat and had someone paddle for him, and he rode up to where the young people sat on the bank. One of the worst experiences of my life was when I tried this with a friend of mine, a rival of mine, as a matter of fact. He was wooing Peg for her hand (I got not only her hand but everything else, but anyway. . . .). Anyway, Reese was to be Simon Peter, and, of course, I was to be Jesus. We had a youth group down at St. Simon's Island, and the river flowed just around a lovely little peninsula there off from the campsite. We made our plans, we had the boat all ready, just up behind the weeds and the sea grass that grew so that they couldn't see us to begin with, but we were to come from behind the bend of the river and to anchor. And I was to unfold to them the great truths of life.

Unfortunately, we hadn't counted on the current of the Frederica River. We edged our way out far enough to be at an appropriate distance from the crowd when we got there, and suddenly we found ourselves swept down the river. As we went by the group, we were cursing and saying things you wouldn't want to say in Sunday School! We were sweating and tearing off our garments. It was just awful!

But not that day. It was not a river; it was the Sea of Galilee, as Luke calls it, the Lake of Gennesaret. And Jesus, pressed by the throng—he could hardly breathe—got into one of the empty boats. It happened to be Simon Peter's, and he asked Simon Peter if he could row him out a distance so that he could speak to the people, and presumably Simon Peter did and took his partners with him.

And Jesus spoke to them for a long time, and then when he had finished speaking, the story goes, you will recall that he told Simon Peter to cast out into the deep. Peter said, "All right," and then Jesus said, "Lower your nets into the sea."

There's a bit of humor here. Jesus the carpenter rabbi is telling Peter the great fisherman how to fish. And Peter responds in a most beautiful and human way, "Master, we have toiled all night long and caught nothing." But then Peter says the magic word, "*Nevertheless.*" "Nevertheless, at your word we will let down the net." And they did, and all of a sudden the boat was all but swamped with the great catch. And they beckoned to their partners James and John, the sons of Zebedee, and they brought their boat out, and their boat filled up.

It was a great fish fry for Capernaum that night, I imagine. It's funny to me that that's not what grabs Peter. He all of a sudden recognizes the wonder and the mystery of a generosity that he had never counted on. And he says a remarkably human thing, "What do you have to do with me? Depart from me. I'm a sinful man." And then the great mystery begins to take place. Notice Jesus does not tell him to *stop* being a sinful man. He tells him to stop being afraid. And that's what he would tell us sinful men, and women, and children. Stop being afraid.

And then he gives them a commission. I will make you fishers of people, and you will catch people. And that's what the great abundance of the fishes was all about, the great abundance of what Peter's life would become:

People not drawn into nets but drawn out of captivity.

That's the wonder and mystery of it all. A lot of us, I suspect, know what it feels like to talk about, "We have toiled all the night long, all the nights, and all the days, and all the weeks. And we have caught nothing." And Jesus in so many words says, "Look at what you see as the hopelessness, and I will show you possibilities."

And when they got back to the shore, they left everything and followed him. Not only because they recognized at last who *he* was, but because they recognized all the possibilities that were in *them* through him and with him. That's a remarkable discovery.

It's funny how God sets us up for things, prepares us for things when we don't know we're being prepared, certainly we don't know what we're being prepared for.

Just a few nights before I got the call from Thomasville that my mother had at last died, we were invited, Peg and I, over to some new friends' house, who suddenly had become old friends. They're both gifted beyond my imagination. He was a great baritone. He doesn't sing anymore because his voice, like some others' I know of, has sort of faded from its elegance. I knew all about this and begged him to let us hear if he had any recordings of his music from those days. He sang professionally; he sang on the City Service Hour that Peg and I used to go out and court by on Sunday evenings although we didn't know it was his voice. And he said, "Oh, yes. I have a few things you might like." And, almost apologetically, he said, "This is a kind of religious one, but I want you to hear it." It was one I had heard many times sung by George Beverly Shea in the Billy Graham crusades. It's a kind of revival song. But as sung by this greatest male voice I think I ever heard, it was setting me up. "I'm a child of the King, *child* of the King, through Jesus my Savior, I'm a child of the King."

And so are you, and so are we all. And in what seems like sometimes desperately unyielding lives, there are great possibilities. And God only knows what you can do for yourself if you remember what my friend reminded me of right before I lost my mother: I'm a child of the King. Amen.

The Great Shoal of Fish

It begins as a fish tale. Peter, James, and John are all there. They were, as you will recall, all fishermen. It was their livelihood. On this occasion, they had fished all night long and had caught nothing.

I can truly identify with that. My father was a passionate fisherman. It, thank God, was not his livelihood, but it was indeed his greatest avocation, his greatest joy in life. He was good at it, too, and gained the admiration of his friends, *except when he took me*. He did his dead-level best to teach me how to fish. But he was no dummy; he first taught me how to paddle the boat. And laying modesty aside, he taught me well. I was one of the best boat paddlers in all of South Georgia by the time I was fifteen years old. But, I was also a kind of Jonah, about a hundred and twenty pounds of bad luck.

Let me interject something here. I have often heard, in the short time I have been your vicar, about these wonderful trips some of you take to Louisiana and other parts south and west, and how many fish you caught and what fun it was. I would just like to say, I AM SICK OF IT! My idea of a great day on the river or on the lake or on the Gulf of Mexico was catching enough fish to feed my Dad and me enough to keep us from starving and having to go to one of those rotten, greasy diners, the only ones available in those miserable parts. (I think that's the main reason I'm skin & bones and walk with a limp. I lost my appetite when I was sixteen years old.) Anyway, I understand about "fishing all night" or all day or all weekend and catching nothing.

But back to the story. Differing from the other Gospels, Luke tells us that Peter, James, and John had been with Jesus for some time. Accordingly, they had witnessed his wondrous works of healing and teaching throughout Galilee. Indeed, they had been associated with him in his role as rabbi. Yet, it is not until this fishing episode, this miraculous *catch*, that they recognize him as *Savior*.

Now, surely Luke is not suggesting that they were unmoved by his healing the greatly afflicted or by his words of wisdom and divine truth and gave all of that lower priority to a boat load of fish. No, indeed! Rather, it is Luke's purpose to reveal to us a glorious truth that most of us have missed along the way, namely, that Jesus comes to us *where we are*, in the ordinary events and moments in our ordinary lives, the places where we hurt, and need, and often find ourselves helpless. And that is precisely where he comes to Peter, James, and John, in their work and in what, for the moment, seemed like its *futility*.

Does that ever get to you? The sort of every-day-ness of things? One of the many reasons I love housewives in particular—the dishes that get washed after breakfast are the same dishes that get washed after lunch and after supper, and the same for the diapers that get changed and the laundry that gets washed and the beds that get made-up, the "same old same old" days without end! I remember the epitaph at the grave of a British washer-woman: "Don't bother me now, don't bother me never. I want to be dead forever and ever!"

The same goes for businessmen too, believe me, the same old office, the same old boss, the same old bottom-line, the same old anxieties about being adequate and about being faithful, responsible providers. The "same-old-same-old" that robs of us of energy and joy and meaning and of God!

Maybe that's what fishing all night and catching nothing felt like to Peter, James, and John. Yet, that is precisely where Jesus finds them.

I remember an old friend Mr. Neal who visited prisoners regularly, and once, in the prison, he asks one of them: "Have you found Jesus?" And the surly answer he got is one of my favorites: *"I didn't know he was lost"!*

I'm not at all sure that we "find Jesus" as much as that Jesus *finds us.*

There is a bit of humor in the moment when Jesus found Peter and James and John. They are old sea dogs whose entire occupation had been fishing. Jesus worked his young life as a carpenter. Yet, he gives them advice. "Try the other side of the boat." You can almost see Peter rolling his eyes and saying, "Right, Boss Man," and murmuring to himself, "Gee, why hadn't we thought of that?" So, halfway to humor the carpenter-turned-*Field & Stream*, he does what he's told.

They got there that day with jobs: they left with *vocations.* Vocation is a wonderful term. It comes from the Latin *vocare*—"to be called." Studs Turkel, in his book *Working,* says: "I think most of us are looking for a calling not just a job. Most of us have jobs that are too small for our spirit. Jobs are not big enough for people."

So what is our calling? It is precisely the same one he gave to those bewildered fishermen, Peter, James, and John: "Do not be afraid; from henceforth you shall be catching men . . . and women and children and tax collectors and harlots and auto-body repairmen and bankers and clerks and housewives and, once in awhile, Episcopal priests." In other words, letting the Christ that is in you reach out and touch the Christ that is in others, and loving them. And a good way to get started is the Gospel according to James, "Baby James Taylor," this time: "Shower the people you love with love, show them the way that you feel, things are gonna' work out better if you only will."

Saints and Naming

One can only imagine how it must have been when, in our history, the first vestry or vestry-to-be sat down with the Bishop, the Right Reverend Somebody or maybe even the Preposterously Reverend Somebody (!) to select the name of the parish to be, this outpost of Christendom, this Part-of-the-Body-of Christ himself, with all the holy and human and heavenly weight of that momentousness—that givenness of things—that comes with *naming*.

Did it have any of the sentiment or excitement or mystery that attended the time when your parents-to-be decided on what they would name you, the person-to-be?

Did they pick St. Margaret's because the parish was well stocked with St. Johns? I have a Presbyterian friend who says the reason he isn't an Episcopalian today is that when he was old enough to decide, the only Episcopal church nearby was "St. Chrysostom's," and he figured that if he couldn't pronounce it, he ought not to join it, and perhaps he was right because the way he pronounced it came out "St. Chrysanthemum."

The church, however named, belongs to Christ and as we all know, "God so loved the world that He gave his only begotten Son"—to whoever would have him! And that means you, me, and the foul smelling vagrant who blows past on an ill wind and the Preposterously Reverend Bishop Somebody.

Think of the *faces* of people who have touched us and whom we have touched. Not just our ancestry, but ourselves, where we've been, where we come from, as near as Clem and as far away as China. Think where their life's blood has reached and their *livingness* has been and come from and gone to, and you have the whole, great globe itself.

To come to our Saint's Day, the one for whom we are named, is to come to something of the power not only of who she was and is, and to the meaning of her name, but also more importantly to the power of who *we* are—and to the meaning of our own names.

"I drew a circle once around me there . . .

I found myself, and that was *everything*."

To find out about St. Margaret is to find out also about *yourself—we who are called to be saints*. And that is, indeed, everything. And to do that is to somehow with God's help and the blessed gift of *memory* to praise him for all the places and all the people and all the life that has touched us. "For all our blessings, known and unknown, remembered and forgotten, we give thee thanks," says an old prayer and it's for the *all but unknown ones and the more than half forgotten ones* that we do well to look back over the journey of our lives because it's *their presence* that makes the life of each of us a sacred journey.

It is not just the saints of the church we should name in our prayers but all the foolish and wise ones, the shy ones and overbearing ones, the broken ones and the whole ones, the despots and crack pots of our lives who in one way or another have been our particular fathers and mothers and saints, and whom we loved without knowing that we loved them and by whom we were helped to whatever little we may ever have or hope to have of some kind of crazy sainthood of our own.

Memory is more than a looking back to a time that is no longer. It's a looking deep into another kind of time altogether, where everything that ever was continues not just *to be*, but to grow and change with a life that's in it still. The people we loved. The people who loved us. The people who taught us things. Dead and gone though they may be, as we come to understand them in new ways, it's as though they come to understand us, and *through them*, we come to understand ourselves in new ways too!

Who knows what the "communion of saints" means, but surely it means more than just that we are all of us haunted by ghosts—because they are not *ghosts*, not dim echoes of voices that have long since ceased to speak, but saints—in the sense that through them, something of the power and goodness of life itself not only touched us once long ago but continues to touch us to this day.

They have their own business to get on with now, I assume, "Increasing in knowledge and love of thee," says the Book of Common Prayer, and "moving from strength to strength," which is business enough for anybody. And one imagines all of us on this shore fading for them as they journey ahead toward whatever new shore awaits them, but it's as though they carry something of us on their way, as we most surely carry something of them on ours.

If they had things to say to us then, they have things to say to us now. Let us remember their names and know our own names as our own.

All Saints Day: A Family Reunion (2000)

Well, here we all are. Welcome to the family reunion. That's what All Saints Day is all about—what every Sunday is all about if we could just halfway believe it. I try to say it as though I believe it, and you respond to it as if you took it for truth. How does it go? "Therefore, we praise you, joining our voices with angels and archangels and all the company of heaven who forever sing this hymn to proclaim the glory of your name." Hmm. And then we sort of do it an injustice with our weakly sung "Holy, Holy, Holy."

"With angels and archangels and all the company of heaven"— which includes everyone who has ever touched you and blessed your life: the great ones and the not so great, the highly remembered and honored and admired and those who have no memorial whatever. And it includes you as you touch and bless the lives of others.

I've told you this about my friend John Porter. Several years past he was on the short list to be interviewed by a great big church in Palisades, California. He wanted very much to think that they might call him there. He was terrified. He had just come through the first stages of recovery as an alcoholic, and he knew that they knew that. He wondered too about his own gifts and his own capacity to serve what he considered something like an aircraft carrier, a huge church out there. And he sort of began to talk himself into not going. In fact, he got right angry with them, so much did he fear rejection. He went to see his sponsor in AA and told him about it, and his sponsor wisely listened, and when John had finished his little diatribe, he

71

said, "Well, John, just let me ask you. Do you feel that you have anything in you to give to others? And John sort of groused around and said, "Well, I certainly hope so." And his sponsor said, "Well, I know so. So why don't you just go out there and touch their lives and let them touch yours and if nothing else comes of it, it will be a worthwhile journey." And so he did. And so they did, and they called someone else, but every now and then he gets a letter from them, and they from him, because it worked.

Angels and archangels and all the company of heaven. Does it ever occur to you that no matter where you go and no matter how lonely you get that you are not alone? Everything that has every touched and blessed your life is not only remembered but is a part of you and goes with you and it is as alive as you are. That's what we're here to celebrate.

What was it that Jesus was blessing in that motley crowd of the poor in spirit and the mournful and the meek and the ones trying to make peace with themselves and with others and the ones hungering for God? What was it in them that he blessed? The same thing that he blesses in you. We know it as faith, however small and frail. We know it as hope, however dimmed and blurred by fear. We know it as love, however reticent and timid at times and however sometimes distorted. That's what he blesses. And he touches our lives with the saints.

Now, Ambrose Bierce has a definition of saints in what he calls his *Devil's Dictionary*. A saint is simply "a dead sinner, revised and edited"! Exactly. Everyone dear to you who has outrun you to the father's house, all the hell they may have given you is swept aside for the beauty you now know to have been in them, revised and edited. And the glory of it all is that you are the edition, and you carry that with you. Some of them, God knows, we've even forgotten their faces, let alone their names. We're not talking about the perfect ones—there was only one of those—we are talking about flesh and blood, the crazy uncles, the God-struck people who however they flubbed up their lives knew that God loved you and that God loved them, and that's the family reunion.

"The gentle guest, the willing host, affection deeply planted / It's strange how we remember most the ones we took for granted." You know? Don't take anyone for granted. In the journey of your life, you have been touched by the saints, for who are the saints but the ones who taught us things, who encouraged us, the happiest ones of all—who made us laugh—and they're not just out there; they're in here. That's the mystical part about me that you may or may not like, but I do believe that when we say those words, we are indeed joining the mighty chorus, and that every step we take, we take with them, we in their spirit, they in ours. We are not alone no matter how much we think that. That doesn't mean that God is always with us in some remote or untranslatable way; it means that he is with us in the life and blood of the beings who touched our lives. However irreligious you may be, you are not alone. You are blessed and touched and kept company by them.

One of the most painful moments in my whole life, let alone my life as a priest, took place about thirty-five or forty miles north of here, up in Cedartown at St. James

Episcopal Church where I was kind of lurking around until you guys came up. It was a small congregation of about thirty-five, not thirty-five families, thirty-five people, so whenever anything happened to anyone, it happened to everyone else. And there was a horrible tragedy in that town, a couple in the parish, and the woman was killed in an automobile accident in her mid-thirties. Her husband was left with two beautiful little children, a boy and a girl. After the tragedy, they stayed away appropriately from company and didn't come to church for a few weeks. But I remember the first Sunday they came back. And the attention of the whole parish was sort of focused on this man and his two little children. And when they came up to the altar to receive the bread and the wine, I heard a voice cry out, and it just shattered me, the little boy: "Where is my mama?" And I prayed to God that he would let me say the right thing. I was tempted to say, "Well, she is with Jesus in heaven." But I didn't. For once, no, for the thousandth time, God came to my rescue, and I said, almost fiercely, "She is right here. Right now. Right here. And don't you forget it." The whole church sort of sobbed, and so did I, but there was a glory in it, a blessing, an honor. And I felt way down in my own tattered soul that I had spoken the truth.

Now we don't do much of this in the Episcopal church—we don't ask people to raise their hands, and I'm not going to ask that of you either. Sometimes I do at meetings ("All those who want to go to the bathroom, raise your hands," that stuff). But I'd like you to raise your heart if this applies to you. *Have you been blessed?* Well, if you have, you have a holy obligation. You were blessed because God simply loves you, is just crazy about you, just the way you are, but you were blessed, also, to *be* a blessing. So why don't you just go out there and do that and be that— as we go out on this wonderful family reunion.

Parable of "The Sower"

Even if they were not our mothers and fathers, the people who told us stories, or who read us books, or who put us to sleep with fairy tales became our mothers and fathers in ways that neither they nor we were probably able to understand at the time and in ways which we can apprehend only in looking back across the years.

I remember my Aunt Elizabeth reading me Bible stories from a big, black, thick book which, at the time, was so heavy I could barely lift it from its honored place on the shelf to her generous and ample lap. And there the book and I would rest as she read me those marvelous tales about David and Goliath, about Moses and the parting of the Red Sea, and about my favorite, Elisha, who was teased by little boys because of his bald head and who, in retaliation, invoked the wrath of Jahweh down on them, which must have worked, because immediately some bears came out of the woods and *ate* them!

From another book, she read me fairy tales: Rumpelstiltskin and Sleeping Beauty and Jack and the Beanstalk and many, many others. Even today I can still remember the wonderful visions with which I curled up in that marvelous old feather bed and went to sleep with dreams of a world too wonderful to describe.

When my aunts weren't around, my Uncle Henry would sometimes volunteer. He was the ne'er-do-well who had married my Aunt Sue Belle. Like Elisha, he was as bald-headed as an egg, but to my deep gratitude was more good-humored about it than the Prophet. It was one of the few things he was good-humored about. He had been a hard-working and totally unsuccessful farmer all of his life and lived constantly under the scornful, scrutinizing, and always critical eye of his wife and her sisters, including my mother. He had a hard life. And for some of the same reasons, so did I, so that some way or another, Uncle Henry and I became silent partners, with a great and saving bond between us. To everybody else he was as sour in disposition as the old pipe that he smoked Prince Albert tobacco in and as blunt and stubby of temper as the cigars he smoked on Sundays.

He has been dead for nearly thirty years, and, like his cigar, long gone to ash. But, I sometimes miss him and think of him as though it were only yesterday that I sat with him on the porch swing and heard his wicked chuckle as he opened the same book of fairy tales that my aunt read from. I was at something like the tender age of six or seven. I remember that I had not yet learned to read myself, but even then I knew that what Uncle Henry read to me somehow didn't even match the pictures, much less the words in the book. You wouldn't believe his version of Goldilocks and the Three Bears! I have forgotten how he fashioned the first part of the tale, but I remember that the ending was not altogether a happy one for Goldilocks. When the bears came home and found that someone had eaten their porridge, broken up part of their furniture, and had lounged around on every bed in the house till she found the one that suited her, they were so incensed that they permitted Junior, the baby bear, to make sport of her and then sold her into slavery! I was too young to understand what "making sport" was all about, but whatever it was, I knew that it wasn't nice. Anyway, the moral, according to Uncle Henry, was never to go uninvited into a bear's house. And I have remembered that well. I never have!

Despite the fact that I would go to bed horrified at the fate of poor Goldilocks, I found that there was a quality in Uncle Henry's tales that was utterly lacking in those of my Aunt Elizabeth, and as soon as I had recovered from the horror of the night before, I would beg him to read more. I remember that my brother very stupidly told my Aunt Sue Belle what Henry had read to us, so for a long time, there were no more stories. But when my aunts were away from the house, he would sneak one in every now and then, and to my great delight he would tell my brother that he couldn't listen because he was a tattle-tale! It was one of the few triumphs of Henry's and mine in those days.

Jesus came telling stories, too, parables, some of them having more the quality of my Uncle Henry's tales than a literary quality. In fact, if Matthew had presented this parable to a college instructor in Creative Writing, he probably would have gotten a D-minus, maybe even an F.

His opening sentence—you know, the one that's supposed to adroitly introduce the subject, or the theme—begins with "A sower went out to sow." And, then, he immediately shifts from that less than exhilarating opener to a description of what happens to the seeds, as they fall rather haphazardly to the ground. And then he begins to talk about the ground, and about the different conditions of the soil whereupon the seeds fell, as sown by the sower who went out to sow and who by now has completely vanished from the story, so that wants to say, "SO[W] what!"

The plot's not all that great either. On the other hand, it does have some good traditional elements to it, not the least of which is a happy ending, arrived at through disappointment and mild suspense. So make it a D-minus.

At the hands of one of my own English teachers, it probably would have gone like this: "The soil lay restive, ill-at-ease, and eager to nourish new life, as the sun crept slowly, furtively, above the rim of night, shedding its golden glow upon the misty haze of a Palestinian morning." That beats "A sower went out to sow," even it does ramble around a bit.

The parable doesn't ramble around very much, and if it dismisses the sower too soon to suit us, it's because he has done his job, and the gist of the matter lies elsewhere, lies somewhere in the soil and the seeds and in what *happens* and *doesn't happen* in what rather haphazardly passes for our lives, and in what happened and didn't happen in the lives of those Galileans who stood haphazardly around and listened when Jesus first told it.

And when he says to them, as he says to us today, "He who has ears to hear, let him hear," we had better listen, for it is our own lives we are listening to.

This rough-hewn little story that begins "A sower went out to sow" is the story of your life. And it's the story of mine. And as much as the English teacher in us would like to touch it up a bit, give it some zest and color—golden glow, and misty haze, the rim of night, and a Palestinian morning—we don't let much of that happen to our lives, so why should we let it happen to the *story* of our lives? The ground is there—the good earth, the soil—we move about on it, we spread it with concrete, we track it in on the carpet. We plot it up, and it feeds us. We put foundations in it, and it supports us. It holds us up. But it also brings us down. What we can see and touch of each other comes from it and goes back to it. Earth to earth—ashes to ashes. And the color and the splendor, the beauty and sheer majesty of it, are most of the time lost to us as we stumble around on it like blind moles, trying desperately to get to the bottom of things.

That's the condition most of us face much of the time. Certainly, it was the condition that those men faced, who first heard the story of their lives. They could hardly catch sight of the splendor of the road, so fearful were they of where the road led, if indeed it led anywhere except back to their own sadness. To such men as did the Savior come to save, you don't talk about babbling brooks and morning splendors as much as you talk about a cup of cold water and a place to lay one's head.

A sower went out to sow.

The function of parables, by the way, lest someone mislead you, is to reconcile opposition, to overcome resistance—the opposition and resistance that exist between the one who tells the tale and those who listen to it. In the New Testament, most of that opposition was provided by the Pharisees, who believed that what Jesus said was too easy, the rest by ordinary run of the mill sinners who believed that it was too hard, and by men without hope who simply believed that it was too good to be true.

What we need to understand is that the Gospel, whether spoken to us in our brokenness or the height of our power, to our poverty or to our great sense of plenty, to our doubt or to our great longing, to our despair or to our sense of pride, it is always *addressed to*, and must be heard *above*, or by some holy grace *through*, our opposition to its truth.

Part of the opposition we carry around within us is the notion that much of our misery is attributable to villains. Like the story of our lives, however, this parable doesn't offer villains. Not the soil. Not the seeds, certainly. Not the rocks or the weeds. And not the sower. And not you either, no matter how much you may want Him or me or somebody to say that, just so that you can feel guilty and desperate and hopeless, which are just other words for resistance, rebellion, and death.

If, however, *above*, or *through*, our native opposition, we hear its truth, we have ears to hear and hear, then the story will simply tell us about the *givenness of things* . . . the way things are, and how in the midst of them, not by running from them, but by being bold enough to accept God's grace to live amidst them, we become fully human, fully His, fully ourselves.

We love. And some of it goes to waste, or at least doesn't find its target. Maybe the target moved just as we set it loose. Maybe there were rocks that we didn't see, just below the surface, or maybe there were weeds that got there through nobody's fault, including the weeds.

But to be human in the world, you have to be in it. To grit your teeth and clinch your fist in order to survive the world at its worst is by that very act to become unable to let something be done to you and in you that is more wonderful still. The trouble with steeling yourself against the harshness of reality is that the very steel which secures you from being destroyed secures you also, I think, from being opened up and transformed by whatever the holy power is that life itself comes from.

You can survive on your own. You can grow strong on your own. You can even prevail on your own, but you cannot, I think, become fully human on your own.

And it seems to me that this is one of the things we find out about in the story of our lives that begins with "A sower went out to sow."

We Have a Law

Simon the Pharisee. He was a fond admirer although, let us say, with a cautious distance. Like a lot of my lonely friends, he had a warm curiosity about him, warm enough to make him bold enough to take the risk to invite this controversial rabbi to dinner. And the story of that dinner is told in all three of the synoptic Gospels. In Matthew and Mark, he is Simon the Leper, in Luke he is Simon the Pharisee—he was probably both.

At any rate, there is something we need to know before we can really appreciate that story. There was a grand tradition in Jewry in Palestine at that time. Whenever a noble gave a feast, and only nobles could afford to give feasts, all of the poor were not only allowed, but also invited. Word was sent out, "Simon is giving dinner for this Jesus of Nazareth. Come and be the audience." And they surrounded the feast and sat on the edges. Now it was not quite as compassionate as we might want to believe. It was not so much as honored guests. It was more like a clean-up committee, and there were some rather humiliating things about the style in which they served dinner to these poor people. Whenever somebody finished a chicken bone or piece of goat, they would toss it over on the floor, and the people would scramble for it. It was not the place you'd want to take a date! I can see you saying, "Hey, Hannah, let's go over and see what Simon will toss us this evening!" But, the truth of the matter, for the poor, it beat going hungry.

And as we remember the story, whether she came as anybody's date or not, there showed up that remarkable woman, a woman who had to have known him before, and the Gospel reveals that to us, who in some wonderful way had been touched and moved and came not so much for the handouts but to see this man again. Standing there by James Mason the Pharisee, just as she does in the movie *Jesus of Nazareth*, by Zeffirelli, she rushes to him and bathes his feet with her tears, and with her long hair, which was a symbol of her sad profession, she dries them, and then she takes an expensive bottle of perfume, and breaks the top off, and pours it on his feet. And in the movie, James Mason's Simon the Pharisee is watching all this with great care. Without anger and without malice, he reaches out and touches Jesus on the shoulder, and he says, "We have a Law." And Jesus to Simon, with no anger in his voice, either, in fact, with a hint of a smile, says, "Simon, let me tell you something. There were two men who borrowed money from a moneylender. One borrowed fifty silver coins, and the other borrowed five hundred, and neither of them could pay it back. And so he canceled the debts of both. Now, Simon, who will love him the more?" And James Mason the Pharisee says, "Yeah, yeah. But we have a Law." And the law said that a woman like that was not fit for Jewry, not fit to be in the presence of God's children. And what Simon, of course, did not know was that she had broken no law, that she, in fact, was in that moment more one of God's children than even perhaps at that moment was Simon. And so Simon says, "We have a Law."

Well, we have a law, too. We not only have a law, but as the recipients of the whole repository of Western tradition, we live by our laws. And they are precious to us. Without them we could not survive as a community of God's people. And Jesus honored that law. If you remember last time, the last word he said to us was, "I have come not to abolish the law, but to fulfill it." And there is not one little curly-q in it that will be erased as long as heaven and earth shall exist. And what he comes to do is not to set it aside but to invest it with the light and the breath that it needs.

Now, many of us, and I myself, get hooked on self-improvement books. Self-improvement books—you've got to love them. The first one I read said, "You've got to learn to get hold of yourself." And so, man, I worked at that. I was going around holding onto myself as hard as I could. And it really began to feel good, and some good things came out of that. But then it sort of wore out, and I got lonely, and sort of started needed improving again. So I bought another book which said, "You've got to let go of yourself." Let go of myself? You might think that that one I loved the most; no, I despise it. It's one of those abominations that Lacey read to us about this morning. You remember that wonderful book called *Selling By Intimidation*? Getting what you want by intimidation. God knows, most of us are intimidated enough by ourselves—who needs to tell us how to practice it on others?

Self-improvement books still abound. *Pulling Your Own Strings*. Not bad. And some of them have wonderfully good and sound advice. And it's good and sound, and it corresponds to exactly what we have heard read this morning. First in the Psalm, "Happy is the man whose way is blameless." Everybody talks about, "Oh, we shouldn't feel guilt. God doesn't want to lay a guilt trip on us." And that's quite true. What God wants is for us not to be guilty. I tell you the best way I know of getting rid of my guilt is not to be guilty. But, most of the time, I feel very guilty. Maybe it's one of the things I have going for me. When I say, "I have not loved him with my whole heart," and "I have not loved my neighbor as I have myself," I am guilty. And then the wonderful lesson from Ecclesiastes, "God has no use for a sinful man." What is the use for a priest to get up here every week saying, "Oh man, if you knew how bad it is for me, if you knew what a rotten guy I am inside?" What use is that guilt? What use does God have for somebody who's not free to love and free to care and free to be?

The great anger our Lord had for the Pharisees was their *obedience*, which they practiced devoutly, so that they could separate themselves from the rest of the world. God has no use for that either. No, he calls us to obedient so that we are free. All this business about the sins of the flesh. All that really means is going home, looking in the mirror, and, in my case, seeing that rather dumb face. You know now there is an organization that caters to the discrimination faced by the beautiful people—I want to form one for just us mediocre folks. And I tell you the discrimination I use against this mediocre self is when I live according to the flesh and look in the mirror and my first word is, "Hi there, stupid." God would say, "Do you mean to tell me, Jim Callahan, that that is all you are, that that explains your life, just a dumb face?" When we label ourselves, whether as fools or as "hey, hey, hey, look at me," do you know how much contempt there is in that? It cuts off any relationship we could have.

The Sermon on the Mount begins, "Blessed are you poor in spirit" who seek and try to be obedient to decent laws so that together we might enter the kingdom of heaven and bid others to enter with us. It's a bidding thing he calls us to do. And, yes, he commands it not because he wants to be tough on you but because he wants you to be free and blessed.

And if he were cast as James Mason, he would say, "Yes, we have a Law, too. It's called Love. Love. Love."

The Body of Christ

Well, this is the third Sunday of the Epiphany, but among the old timers, it's called Body Parts Sunday, in which Paul goes in this long and rather embarrassing detail about the eyes, the nose, and the ears, and all those unspeakable body parts and how they are all one. And then he concludes by saying, "You are the body of Christ."

If one suffers, we all suffer; if one rejoices, we all rejoice. Wonderful news. Shocking news. You. Not the guy next to you. You. Not the guy in the funny suit. You . . . are the body of Christ. And what does a body do?

Well, when Jesus went home for the first time since his fame had begun to spread through all of Galilee, he's asked to take the role of the lay reader and to stand and read the lesson, and they hand him the scroll, the book of Isaiah, but he selects the passage. "The spirit of the Lord God is upon me, for he has anointed me to preach good news to the poor, to proclaim release to the captives and recovering of sight to the blind, to set at liberty those who are oppressed and to proclaim the acceptable year of the Lord" (whatever that may mean). And then he closed the book, and he sat down. And all eyes were fixed on him, and they were greatly moved—not only by the words but by his speaking them—and then he said that shocking news. "This day," not tomorrow, not the hereafter, but "this day this scripture is fulfilled in your hearing."

And so he proclaimed and laid claim to the role Isaiah had given to the Messiah. That's all beautiful and wonderful to contemplate. It makes great music, it makes great hymns, it makes great poetry and understanding. But it also makes something else. It conveys to you what your role is, too. This is the awful thing about the New Testament. *Nothing ever happened to Jesus that will not happen to you.* That's both the good news and the bad news. And we'll find out the real part of the bad news next Sunday. But this is today, and we must talk about our Lord's priorities for himself and for you and me, who are his body.

To proclaim good news to the poor. God knows they could use some these days, couldn't they? Good news to the poor. Release to the captive. God knows there are enough of us who are captive, mostly to our own fear. Recovering of sight to the blind and setting at liberty those who are oppressed. Somewhere in there, pal, you and I reside.

So what does this all mean? This weekend, yesterday, I buried a very dear old friend of mine, somebody closer to me than I even began to know till I faced that painful task. His name is Dick, Dick Hackney. He was a man of great reserve who kept his own counsel. He was a man who loved the Earth, who dug in it, planted in it, reared garden after garden. His one enemy in all the world was morning glories which took over whenever it rained. And I had the great joy of standing before his family and friends and saying, "Thank God, the morning glories won." I talked about what Jesus said when his best friend died and his sisters came out to greet Jesus, and they said, "If you had been here, Lord, he would not have died. Oh, we know that he will rise again in the Resurrection." And Jesus interrupted them and said, "I am the Resurrection. He that believeth in me, even if he is dead, yet shall he liveth. And whosoever liveth (and here's the key word), whosoever liveth and believeth in me shall never die." That's what I went up there to talk about, that dear man in all of his goodness, all of his unselfishness, all of his kindness and grace and mercy, though he never darkened the doors of the church. And when I heard the other preacher who was the preacher of the church that he should have darkened, when I heard him talk about "Death and how we better all be ready for it," and I'm up there standing and saying "There ain't no Death," kind of a contest, you see, then I understood why old Captain Dick didn't bother much to go to church where they sort of apologized to God *for him* and talked about God's inclusiveness, that maybe, *maybe*, with any luck at all and with his wife's devotion to God, he might just possibly sneak in. And I thought, God help us all. Jesus doesn't give a rip about what you believe or don't believe. He that liveth in me . . . shall never die. Just that simple. And what does that mean? I think it has a lot to do with theology. I think it has a lot to do with grace. Being kind and merciful and gentle, bringing light in to people's lives. If it doesn't mean that, I don't know what else it could mean.

Some of you have been around long enough to remember a little dining establishment, a little café down here on the Bankhead Highway where Holmes Road comes in. There was a dreadful little place down there called Gene's Dine-o-Mite, ok? I used to go in there every day. My stomach suffered for years following, but I would go in and order the special of the day, which was always kind of a, if you'll pardon the expression, kind of a gut bomb. And I would sit there and eat if for no other reason than the old lady behind the counter who would say, "Hey, darling, how you today, darling, good to see you, darling, what are you gonna have today, darling?" It made my day. Nobody calls me that, not even, least of all, Peg. It was just good to go down there and let a little sunshine in, even if I had to pay for it in a gastrointestinal way.

The woman at the check-out counter down at the K-mart, underpaid, treated badly most of the time, she finds a way of saying hello to you and being gracious to you and kind of has, I think, much to do with living in Him.

The one thing I hate about the Irish genes in me is the quick temper, the word that hurts and stings like a wasp. I have a cure for it, now, believe it or not. It's a little prayer I wrote; it rhymes. "Gentle me, Lord Jesus and ever keep me kind. And keep me there for others that I am kept as thine."

That's what matters, pal. The light and the grace and the kindness that comes out of the love of Jesus that comes into our hearts. I find to my consternation that it used to be that God was forever restoring my faith in mankind. Now, I find that mankind is forever restoring my faith in God. And old Captain Dick was one of those, though he didn't have a membership card.

I remembered, thank goodness, something that Peter says in that great sermon that he preaches in the tenth chapter of the Book of Acts. "I perceive," he says, "that God shows no partiality and that in every nation anyone who fears God and does good is acceptable to Him." Sounds pretty good to me.

I've been reading a man named Cormac McCarthy; one of you put me on to him. The one I read first is called *All the Pretty Horses*. He is sort of a new William Faulkner, and the landscape is bleak, and the lives of his characters kind of bleak. But this is an adventure story about two lads who, when the youngest of them suffers the death of his grandfather (that's the only tie he has with his family and with his community), they get out of Dodge and go over the river to Mexico, and there begins a frightful adventure. They end up working as horsemen, and they are greatly gifted at that. They end up on a hacienda. The hero of the story falls in love with the daughter of the hacienda owner—what else would you expect? But then they are accused of a crime they did not commit, in fact, a crime that did not happen. And all of sudden, they become brutalized and put in prison and treated more like animals than human beings.

It's an awful story.

Finally, the aunt of his sweetheart buys them out of jail and promises that her niece will never see him again. But they don't know that.

So they're on their way back to the hacienda and while they're hitchhiking, in pain from the beatings they suffered, but glad to be out of there, they get on the back of a flatbed truck. And after a while, the flatbed truck stops for five farmworkers. They get on, too. "They're very circumspect," says the author, "they're very courteous." They're interested in who these men are. "Where do you come from?" From Texas. "Ah, de Texas. Very good." The young man has on a new suit, and he says in Spanish, "Are you going to see your sweetheart?" And the hero says, "Yes, that's true." "Ah, que bueno. How good, how good." And they all smile. And then the author says,

"After, and for a long time to come, he would have reason to recall both the recollection of those smiles and to reflect upon the good will that provoked them for it has the power to protect, and to confer honor and to strengthen resolve, and to heal men and women and bring them to safety after all other refuges and sources have been exhausted."

Wonderful. Let your life be made out of that which is protective and which confers honor and strengthens resolve and heals men and women and brings them to safety for of such is the kingdom of God.

Who Do You Say I Am?

I don't know if you've noticed it or not, but this passage, this episode in our Lord's ministry, comes up at least three times. Perhaps the church fathers deemed it that urgent. The story of how our Lord, having sent his twelve out for the first time on their own, sent them out to preach and to teach and to heal, and as it is accounted in each of the gospels, they come back rejoicing at the success they have experienced and how well things went. And Jesus is greatly elated and encouraged by this, intervenes at the feeding of the five thousand, and they draw aside for a rest, and Jesus, having sent them out, asks the question that would seem natural, "What are the people saying? Who do they think I am?"

And they answer very eagerly because they had been fascinated by what they had heard. "Some say that you are John the Baptist returned from the dead." And there was good substance to that because John the Baptist proclaimed the same theme that our Lord adopted—believe, for your salvation is at hand. They preached the same word, and they were kinsman, and it was likely that they would be associated. But he was more than John the Baptist, different from John the Baptist. As I have said to you before, John the Baptist was my mother in drag, and maybe yours too. John the Baptist was full of anger with all of the people of Israel. He demanded that they come out for him; he lived alone, a monkish life, and they had to come to him; he neither ate unreasonably nor drank any fruit of the vine. Jesus, on the other hand, ate and drank cheerfully and often in very dubious company. Very great differences. When John the Baptist talked about repentance, it was not only a turning away from your sins, but a turning away from yourself. When Jesus preached it, it meant, "Look this way. Look into my face and know that you are forgiven." He was more than John the Baptist.

"Some say that you are Elijah." Now, there was an interesting association. Elijah the miracle worker, the mighty prophet. Unfortunately, Elijah and his first cousin whose name is so much like his that many think they were the same people, their miracles were often, if you'll forgive the French, just for the hell of it. Make the anvil float on the river just for the fun of it, you know. Jesus' miracles were always a response of compassion. He didn't make anything float on the water but himself to see if Peter trusted him. He healed broken bodies and broken hearts. His miracles were miracles of grace and compassion, so he was more than Elijah.

"Some say that you are one of the ancient prophets, like Moses the Lawgiver." There was substance in that too, although he didn't give as many. He gave one, as you recall. "This is my commandment, that you love one another as I have loved you." Lawgiver but only insofar as there is a law in the heart that loves and forgets not.

So when they reported all that, I'm sure that Jesus was impressed. "That's interesting." And then he asks the all-important question, and maybe that's why the church fathers put it in the text so many times. "Who do *you* find me to be? Who am I *to you?*" he said. Peter spoke for them all. "You are the closest thing to God we will ever know.

You are the Christ. You are the Messiah." And Jesus said, "Yes. Good. Now don't tell anybody this for awhile because the Christ you are talking about is one who must suffer many things before anyone will recognize him, including yourselves, as the Messiah."

So what do we do with this? First of all, I think we understand it for what it is. It was not a hide and seek game: Guess who I am, and if you guess right, Allah will grant your wish. Say the magic word, and out will come the duck with a silver dollar. No. It wasn't that kind of a game.

How do you perceive me? What am I to you, each of you? When Diedrich Bonhoeffer was about to die, the great Lutheran pastor, the great martyr of World War II in Germany, in the prison where he and others like him, the seven thousand who had not bowed to Hitler, the seven thousand Christians, as he waited there in the prison hearing the Allies, hearing the sounds of the bombs as they were dropped on the city, not knowing that deliverance was about to take place, he had no sense that he was going to be spared, and so he wrote from prison, this interesting question. Who is Jesus Christ to us in this day and at this time? He did not expect a miracle. He did not expect Elijah. He did not expect anything except to die at the hands of his executioner. Who is Jesus Christ today, he said, and that question echoes down across the decades, down to you and me, to this day.

Who is he to you? Remember the old Lewis Grizzard story, the man he set behind on the plane, and he sort of shocked him by saying to Lewis, "Do you know the Lord?" And Lewis Grizzard said, "I know about him." And that's the answer most of us would give, we know about him, we know of him, we know the things that are said, we've read a lot of the stuff that is written. But any sense of *who* he is, any kind of notion of one who addresses *me*, is maybe kind of foreign to some of us. I don't know what picture hangs in your heart if any picture at all.

I remember my friend John Porter was visiting a little girl in a mental hospital. She had been the victim of the worst assault a child could possibly know at the hands of one of her kinsmen. And she was like so many victims of that kind of assault; she felt dirty and guilty. When John went to see her in this Catholic hospital place, there was a picture of the sacred heart of Jesus at the bedside table, and she started crying. She said, "I wish you would take that picture down because it makes me ashamed." And he said, "Who do you think the picture is?" And she said, "Jesus." And he said, "Oh, no. I'll be glad to take it down, but it's not Jesus. Jesus will have nothing to do with your shame. So if you have a picture of somebody that makes you feel ashamed, it ain't Jesus. Ok? That much I know." I think he would have you perceive him as that which he most longs to be for you. Your friend, your companion along the way, the one who encourages you, the one who really wants to see you have a great time, always there, whether you see him or not.

Who is he to you? Right now, right here. It is worthy of your deepest thought and prayer.

Blind Man Healed: Let Go and Let God

All of the lessons we've heard over the past few Sundays have come from the time when Jesus had set his face toward Jerusalem, which meant toward the final solution, if you please, meant imprisonment, and crucifixion, and death, and resurrection. So we listen carefully because these are critical and crucial times. The disciples, if you've paid any attention at all, have been largely deaf to what he has said, and blind to what he showed them, so what would be more appropriate in the last leg of the journey than for him to heal a blind man.

Bartimaeus, the son of Timaeus, is standing on the roadside. He has heard that the teacher, the healer, is coming through Jericho, and he hears the stir of the crowd, and he realizes that it must be the teacher, and so with great abandon, he cries out, "Son of David, have mercy on me." The crowd tells him to shut up. He pays them no attention, and says even louder, "Son of David, have mercy on me." And Jesus stops in his tracks, and he says, "Tell him to come here," and the crowd takes a different turn, and they say, "Heed. Take heart, take heart, he's calling you. Come." And so Bartimaeus comes, and he does something very significant. He leaves his cloak on the ground. He tosses it off. Now you need to know about cloaks and their importance in Jewry of the time of our Lord. It was one's most prized possession. It was not only protection against the elements. It was a part of your identity; it was your only security against the outside world, but this man just drops it. Now think about it. A blind man who knows that if it doesn't work, he's gonna lose his cloak, too. The same way you might leave your car running to go into an inner city store and go in to do a little shopping. Not very likely you would find it waiting for you when you got back.

But it's that kind of "something" that he had that made Jesus just love him, take great delight in him. And Mark calls it your faith, "Your faith has made you well." Isn't it interesting that when he comes up to Jesus, Jesus says, "What do you want me to do for you?" The same question he asked James and John last week in reference to their coy, little, stupid desire to sit on his right and on his left. But here comes a man with a much more urgent need, a much more obvious, clearly known need. "What do you want me to do for you?" Now as between one who was widely known and greatly admired for his power to heal and one who was widely known and greatly pitied for his stumbling into the furniture and bumping his way into the traffic because he was blind as a bat, it seems like the question might be something of a taunt. Sort of like if I came up to you, my clothes on fire, and you said, "Is there anything I can do to help you?" Sounds like a taunt. But not so. Jesus wanted Bartimaeus to hear himself *ask* for what his heart so greatly desired so that he would realize how God is about to meet that desire, just as he wants to hear it from you and me: "What do you want me to do for you?"

Moreover, he had already seen what Bartimaeus brought with him, saw it with the cloak lying in the dust, saw the power not just of his faith—for us, faith means, unfortunately, a belief system. Right. That and about two dollars and a half will get you a cup of coffee at the Ritz—

no, it was his trust. It was his surrender. Does that ring a bell with you? The kind of surrender we just sang: "Just as I am, I come." Not to get you up to the altar and get you to join the church, but to get you up to the plate and let you take a swing at whatever stands between you and the fullness of life that the Gospel offers you. Whatever stands between you and every impotent idolatry that you trust and that I trust—all our stuff, all our power, all our imagined self-sufficiency. Take a swing at that. And trust him.

I told you this before, at least some of you, a long time ago. I went off to a clergy conference. The platform speaker for the weekend was an Anglican monk, an Episcopal monk (did you know that we have Episcopal monks?). He was from a brotherhood, and he had come down to talk to us about spiritual growth. And I have to confess to you that I went there as I usually go to big meetings, especially clergy meetings, with a little bit of reluctance, even with a bit of a chip on my shoulder. I didn't want to be there. I wanted to be back here. But, I listened attentively to this dear and gentle, kind man, and in his conversation, he kept using one phrase, a metaphor, over and over again, "Let go and let God." Well, he said that a number of times, and finally, in a little bit of pique, and a little bit of showing off, when it came question and answer time, I said, "Sir, you kept telling us to let go and let God. May I ask you: Let God what?" And he was so kind. He said, "Oh, thank you for that fair and legitimate question. I've been presumptuous in my language." He almost apologized, and then he said, "Let go and let God . . . love you." And I said, "Oh."

I heard a funny story this morning. It was Disability
Sunday at the Presbyterian Church in Atlanta, and they had
some disabled people at the pulpit, and they were just
wonderful. The last one was a woman who runs the whole
Presbyterian institution for disabled persons, and she was
talking about some of her people, some of the people in her
office, some of the beneficiaries of that wonderful service.
And she told about Louey, Louey who can't remember
numbers, and he doesn't write well, but he loves to answer
the telephone. Now her name is Sue. And every now and
then, Louey would get a call, and the person would say,
"May I speak to Sue?" And he would say, "How did you
come to meet Sue?" And the person would realize what
agency she had called, and she would say, "Oh I met Sue at
a retreat or a conference or we talked on the phone."
Louey would say, "Oh, good. What do you want to talk to
her about?" And the person might say, "Oh, I need to
know when she is going to arrive in Philadelphia." And then
Louey might say, "Well, she's not here." "Well, will you
please give her the message?" "I'll try." And then he would
start writing, and he had about three out of the ten numbers
right. But when Sue got back, and he started telling her
about this person and how they had met, she pretty well
knew whom to call back! And it was just wonderful. One
day, Joe, the number two man in the agency, went out of
town and he placed a collect call to the office, and Louey
was manning the phone. The operator said, "I have a
collect call from Mr. Joe Williams to anyone who is there.
Will you accept the call?" And he said, "I can't. Joe is not
here." And she said, "No, no. It's Mr. Joe Williams who's

calling anyone there. Will you speak to him?" And he said, "I can't. Joe's not here." And, then, finally, Joe interrupted and spoke and said, 'Louey, it's me, Joe. Talk to me." And, then, the operator said, "If you want to refuse the call, it's perfectly all right." And then there was a long pause, and finally Louey said, "Joe! I'm so glad to talk to you! There's a call here for you!"

Oh yeah. Oh yeah. There's a call here for you, too, and for me: to let go and let God love you. And to trust him so that you may look beyond what you merely see and listen beyond what you merely hear. And finally get around to knowing you, yourself, and the treasure you are to your God.

Intervention

Jesus, says, if your brother sins, go to him privately and tell him what's wrong, and if he listens to you, then you have gained your brother; if he doesn't listen, get two or three witnesses to come, on his behalf as well as yours, and if he doesn't listen, then he is as a Gentile or a tax collector. That means he is of his own volition to be treated from now on as an outsider, not to be mistreated, not to be judged, not to be condemned, but to be dealt with.

Now, this doesn't sound so much like a reading for the baptism of a little kid. It sounds like a page out of the Vestry Handbook, how to deal with all kinds of people in the church. But that's not what it's about at all. The explanation of what it is all about comes just before this with two scenes. The first is that one of the disciples asks Jesus, in the beginning of this chapter of Matthew, "Who is greatest in the kingdom of Heaven?" And without batting an eye, Jesus turned around and saw a child in the crowd, and he called the child to come to him, and the child did, and he said to his disciples, "Whoever does not become as a little child shall not enter the kingdom of Heaven. But whoever humbles himself as this little child is the greatest in the kingdom of Heaven." So put that in your hymnbook and hum it.

And, then, he tells this little story called the parable of the lost sheep. One shepherd had a hundred sheep, and one of them strayed off and was lost. And he left the ninety-nine and went after the one sheep, and when he found it, he brought it home, and there was much rejoicing.

And then, and then only after these two stories, does he say, "If your brother sins, go to him privately."

God knows, dears, this is not a prescription for constructive criticism. I have never heard criticism that was constructive. The language I hate to hear most of all is the sentence that begins, *"The trouble with you, Jim, is..."* You know? Nobody needs that, nobody wants that, nobody has a right to dump that all on another sinful brother like the rest of us.

It's kind of interesting to me, and it may be a little bit shocking to you, but in all the writings of St. Paul and in all of the Gospels, there is essentially only one sin. It's not your little peccadillos, it's not what's going on between you and your secretary, it's not any of that stuff—it is the sin of unbelief. Jesus hated it.

So what it really sounds like to me is that if your brother is tired, and if he has separated himself from you, from us, go to him, listen to him, give it a chance. Yeah, I think that's it.

It may be about the modern syndrome of intervention. Man, I would hate to walk into a room and see a couple of you, I would hate to see the vestry coming up my sidewalk, I would hate to see the camera crew of *Sixty Minutes* outside the rectory. But there are interventions that work. One story. My friend, my colleague, my inspiration John Porter got a call from the Bishop one day, asking him to come to his office on Thursday at four o'clock. And you never say no to the Bishop, so he assured him he would clear his calendar and be there. And the Bishop said, "I look forward to seeing you, John." And

John put down the phone, and he said he felt a little bit excited. Maybe there was some big opportunity that the Bishop wanted to share with John. So he went with some excitement, and when he went in the Bishop's office, there he saw the Bishop, three of his priest friends, and his wife, and his son, and his daughter, and a representative from Ridgeview Hospital. They talked to him about his drinking—"*The trouble with you, John, is…..*" And he confessed to me that his first response to this was anger, fury, that he felt betrayed. He said, "When my colleagues spoke up, I wanted to say, 'You hypocrites.' When my wife spoke up, I wanted to say, 'You want to take me to the Sobriety Police? Let's take us to the Marriage Police.'" And he was just furious until he heard his daughter say, "Daddy, I love you and I want you well. Please." And he said okay.

Wherever our brother is, whatever he struggles with, Christ is in the midst of it, and we are in the midst of it. And that's what this story is about. That's what the whole Gospel is about. That's what you're about and what I'm about when we acknowledge God.

Jim's Final St. Margaret's Day Sermon   Nov. 12, 2000

St. Margaret's Day, this one a very special one for me. If you've been around these parts for a couple or three St. Margaret's Days, you probably remember well the wonderful story of that pearl of a girl, which is sort of a play on words because the name Margaret means "pearl." And a pearl of a girl she was.   She flunked all the tests for sainthood.   She was not a virgin. She bore into this world eight children. She was not a martyr. She died in her bed from natural causes with a broken heart.   She was sainted not because of her bravery although brave she was, and not because of her piety though few in her time were more devout.   She was sainted by Mother Church because of her compassion—because of her care for the poor and the downtrodden and the needy and the broken.   All those wonderful stories of the mercy that she and her now tamed Malcolm performed, feeding all the poor in the kingdom in the palace every day that they were there, serving the hot meals themselves.   Beautiful stuff.

More, the intimate story of the remnants of St. Margaret's stone which is still there amid the ruins of the old palace, where Margaret was alleged to suckle the children of mothers who were too poor and too underfed to nurture their own children. Now, that's not as implausible as it sounds. Being the mother of eight, she spent a great of her adult life in a kind of milk-giving way, if you please.   It is told to me that she is also the patron saint of Mathis Dairy! Whatever.   All these beautiful little tapestries, probably greatly exaggerated, but nonetheless, we all cynically know

106

that where there's smoke, there's got to be fire. And there was something very special in her, willing to give of herself, of the blessings in her and Malcolm's lives to those who were in great need. There were no miracles attributed to her during her lifetime or to her relics after her death. She was remembered for the miracle that *she* was.

Now, when I came here nearly nineteen years ago, I found to my great delight that there were some people in this great parish who took her rather seriously, whether they were conscious of it or not. I heard about a couple of rogues who had formed a little organization called People for People. They would learn of somebody in need, someone who was in want, and they would get together and raise money and send this person a cashier's check, anonymously, that kind of thing. Well, they began to share this with me, and they would come by and ask me if I knew of any candidates, and, of course, I always did. Any priest halfway worth his salt always would. And I would tell them, and they would do something about it, and soon to my amazement they entrusted me with sort of the management of this fund, and thus was born St. Margaret's Emergency Fund. And, then, others of like mind joined, and this was the great joy, that this same generous spirit was invested throughout this whole parish, and soon the money was coming in and going out, not only to people outside the parish but people within whose problems were embarrassing and hurtful and who were in great need.

Well, one thing led to another. I came here from St. James up in Cedartown, and just before I left that place, we had formed a Soup Kitchen with the aid of some other churches. We had gotten together and had begun to make it work. I remember, on that board, there were some of my own people at St. James, of course, and there was also a dear lady whose name was Mary. She was gentle and kind and gracious, and she declared her full commitment to this cause. But she wanted to know if there were any way we might be able to determine who would be, as she put it, "worthy." Who would be "worthy"? Well, the members of my flock sort of rolled their eyes into the backs of their heads, and one of them gently spoke, and said, "Father Callahan, I wonder if you would address this issue?" And I said, "Yes ma'am, I'll be glad to. Mary, we have already determined on Biblical grounds who will be 'worthy.' If you are hungry, if you are poor, if you are in need, then you are, according to our Lord, worthy." And she said, "Oh, I see."

Well, when I got down here, I began to discuss this with a couple of lapsed Lutherans. I like that term—lapsed Lutherans! The subject came up, and we discussed it with their pastor, one young man of God named Greg Kaufman, and if there ever was a man of God, he is. Greg was keen on this subject too, and then we called in another brother, Dr. Tom Ballard from the Presbyterian church, and soon "the little kitchen of St. Margaret's" became a kind of chuckhouse for every hungry man and woman who could find his or her way to this place. I think the first five days of the first month that we served, there were about thirty-five one day, forty the next, and then it began to build. And then, the Baptists got wind of it. And they sure didn't want to be outdone by a little bunch of Episcopalians and Presbyterians, and so they joined in, and you know the story. Today, that same soup kitchen serves thousands every month. Then, there came along the idea of the community shelter, and you know that story, too.

And dear old St. Margaret's was right in the thick of all of it, sticking her beautiful little nose into the messiness of God's business. And wearing the tattered cloak of doom and finding it becoming. And that's the St. Margaret I want to celebrate today. In fact, it's the one, either consciously or unconsciously, I've been celebrating for a great chunk of my life.

You are a wonderful people, and this is a beautiful family of God's folks. And you belie every one of the tired old jokes, you know the ones.

"The Methodists get 'em out of the gutter, the Baptists wash them off, the Presbyterians introduce them to higher education, the Episcopalians introduce them to high society, and then the Methodists have to get them out of the gutter again."

Right. But you know, I think the current has come full circle. I notice that in urban centers a lot of our Protestant brothers and sisters are moving out into the suburbs and building beautiful colonial churches with tall columns. There are occasions, I'm sure, when that is utterly justifiable, when they are simply following the centers of population whom they want and wish to serve, and I understand that. But I tell you that I am proud of the Episcopal church I know of in urban centers where they are still gutting it out in the inner city right in the midst of Hell's Kitchen.

I'm proud of the churches in this city, too, the Methodist up the street and the Baptist just up the street and the Christian and the Presbyterian church all sticking right here in downtown Carrollville, where the action is. And so are you, my dears.

And one of my requests for you is to try when we build a beautiful new arm to this beautiful St. Margaret's, that you will keep it right where it needs to be, where people know how to get to us. It's not always fun, believe me. Sometimes, the church office over at the Gable House looks more like the Greyhound bus station in St. Louis, Missouri. It's not easy for Julie, much less for Barry, but there they are. And there you are. And there we are.

And, do you know what is your crowning glory? I discovered it a long, long time ago. One day I was in the church office. I'd gotten here early for a change, and the phone rang, and I answered it. "St. Margaret's." And there was a little pause, and then I heard, "Is dis de church that helps people?" I felt the tears hot in my eyes, and I said, "Yes ma'am, it sure is, and what can we do for you?" And we talked, and things got done. And when I hung up the phone, I thought, "You lucky dog. You lucky, lucky dog—just to be a part of this family of God's people." It's because of who you are that I am so honored to be a part of who we are.

Now let's get real, okay?

{in falsetto} "Yes, this is my last St. Margaret's Sunday here."

And I'm trying to be silly about it because way down inside of me, my heart is just, is just weeping. There are about seven more to go, pals.

And now we *could* do something that people do when they know they are going to part. Have you ever been around your spouse when he was about to take off for New York City and stay up there a couple of weeks, and you found yourself getting in a good, fat, rich argument with him so his leaving wouldn't be half so painful? Do you know how that goes? But, now, there's another way of doing it. It's called avoidance. You know. For God's sake, please don't avoid me. I am a very sensitive person, okay? I want us to make these seven last Sundays a glorious, wonderful welcome to what the future holds for you and the challenge that God put in your hearts a long time before you even knew my name. That is what he expects of you, it's what I expect of you, and what I want to be able to empower in you. Let me try my best to do that.

"Is dis de church that helps people?" Yes. And you put that in your hymn book and hum it;

Baptism of William Lawrence Crafton

Today I am choosing to use the Baptismal lesson of Mark 10: 13-16: "They were bringing children to him, that he might touch them; and the disciples rebuked them. But when Jesus saw it, he was indignant, and said to them, 'Let the children come to me, do not hinder them; for to such belongs the kingdom of God. Truly, I say to you, whoever does not receive the kingdom of God like a child shall not enter it.' And he took them in his arms and blessed them, laying his hands upon them."

Now, just to be clear, the appointed lessons for today conclude with what many regard as the most difficult and incomprehensible sayings of Jesus, found in Luke's Gospel: "If any one comes to me and does not hate his own father and mother and wife and children and brothers and sisters, yes, and even his own life, he cannot be my disciple."

So much for family values!

There are two easy ways out:

(1) To point out to all the troops that, of course, that was not what he meant at all and that an understanding of the Greek and Aramaic would explain that what he *really* meant was that we should spend more quality time with our relatives, our postman, the next-door neighbors and our cat; "Did somebody say 'McDonalds'?"

That would be the easy way out if all of you were dolts and if I were dumb enough and careless enough about my own soul to try to take advantage of your gullibility. I would point out, in passing, however, that the word "hate" in the Aramaic does not indicate an emotion. It indicates an act and means what we mean in English by "subordinate" or by "forsake."

What it all boils down to, however, is the simple, clear truth that no loyalty on earth, no affection, no emotional tie can be allowed to stand between us and God.

On the other hand, things get complicated by our deep convictions about love, convictions borne out of the same Gospel as the above--about loving one's neighbor as one's self—about God *being* love—and that when we love anyone, it is of God and God is in it and in it we become participants in God's kingdom. And there's also the business about "Greater love hath no man than this, that a man lay down his life for his friends." All very complicated and complex, because life is rather complicated and complex, and so are we.

At any rate, that would be an easy way out—to explain it away.

(2) The other way out, however, is even an easier one and that is to simply set it aside and use another lesson. This is not only the easy way out, but it is also permissible, since at the 11:00 o'clock service, we are baptizing a little lad named William Lawrence Crafton.

So we go back to the tenth chapter of Mark. Let's hear it again.

"They were bringing children to him, that he might touch them; and the disciples rebuked them. But when Jesus saw it, he was indignant, and said to them, 'Let the children come to me, do not hinder them; for to such belongs the kingdom of God. Truly, I say to you, whoever does not receive the kingdom of God like a child shall not enter it.' And he took them in his arms and blessed them, laying his hands upon them."

So, we all know the story, made dear to us from Sunday School days: People are bringing their children to Jesus to have him touch or bless them. The disciples are irritated by this and try to put a stop to it. Now, let's pause right there a moment. Is this just another episode wherein we get a peek at how dumb and dense these disciples are until they finally see the light? That, too, would be an easy way out. Unfortunately, it would not be the truth. The truth is that they responded this way not because they were hard-hearted or callous or dumb or insensitive. They responded this way because they were Jewish, because they were as trapped as most of us are in the culture in which they lived and in which they had been reared; and in that culture, children were at the very bottom of the food-chain: nothing / nada / zilch. Their response was much more orthodox than Jesus.' For the disciples, the event had about the same effect as the people's bringing their Chihuahua's or their goldfish. There was just no time for such foolishness.

I remember in my early days in Dudley, Georgia, the new, young Baptist preacher in town called on me in great perplexity. It seems that one of his flock, the head deacon and also the president of the bank and mayor of Dudley, had requested that the next Sunday he and his rather imposing, industrial-sized wife wanted to bring "Muffin," their pint-sized Pekingese, to church. It was Muffin's birthday. They also wanted the choir and the congregation to join in singing "Happy Birthday" to Muffin.

Trying hard to keep a straight face, I inquired as to just when in the service did they want this done, whether Muffin was house-trained, and a few other minor technicalities. Sensitively, I asked if he had any idea as to how Muffin, herself, felt about all this. Then we got down to the realities: I asked if he had any reading on how his congregation might feel about the matter. I asked also if he felt that he might lose any members in the process, and he said one or two, maybe. I asked, then, the deciding question. Who would you rather lose, one or two disgruntled sore-heads or your head deacon, president of the bank and mayor of the town? He yielded, of course, to my cold logic. Then, in brotherly love, I asked him if he would mind if I called off my services that day and brought my whole crowd over, not wanting to miss this for all the tea in China!

Well, it all came off. They did indeed sing "Happy Birthday" to Muffin, and no one left the church. I marked the calendar well, assured that this would become an annual event. But God intervened and called Muffin home a couple of months later by way of an unloaded logging truck, rolling through downtown Dudley at about eighty miles an hour. At any rate, the disciples felt about the bringing of the children the same way I first felt about singing "Happy Birthday" to Muffin in a Sunday service. And, ironically, Jesus felt the same way toward the disciples as that poor, bewildered Baptist preacher must have felt about me and my smug enjoyment of his dilemma. He was indignant.

Involved in this tender little scene, which we have a tendency to sentimentalize, is a very profound and shatteringly important issue: The disciples are put off by the fact that whoever brought these children were violating the *purity of faith*. To have children touched and blessed is to reduce blessing, healing, saving, to a kind of magic, so they thought. Is not the idea that the simple touch can mediate miraculous divine power, even without faith, indicative of belief in magic?

That, I think, was the real issue for the disciples. They were standing on principle, as most of us are most of the time, and finding it to be pretty solid ground. What it boils down to is that we tend to believe that God's grace, God's acceptance, God's Kingdom really has to be *earned*, either in some kind of ledger, some kind of bookkeeping in which our good deeds outweigh our bad deeds, or by a faith that has a firm grasp of things, including God's will, and that sooner or later will reform us and get us right and make us really rotten sorry about all the bad things we've felt and thought and done.

The great irony of the situation is that the disciples sought to prevent this "sacrilege" on the very grounds of which Jesus found it utterly beautiful, namely, that the children are blessed just because they have nothing to show for themselves. They cannot count on any achievements of their own; their hands are empty like those of a beggar.

And the good news is that Jesus goes on to enlarge the promise to include everyone. With an authority such as only God can claim, he promises the Kingdom to all whose faith resembles the empty hand of the beggar. And that, I think, is precisely what Jesus means when he says, "Whoever does not receive the Kingdom of God like a child will never enter it." And notice the predicate: "*receive*"!

The Kingdom of God is not something you and I build or bring into being by our good works or our pure faith. The Kingdom of God is something that is, that has been, and that ever shall be, finding its ultimate expression in Jesus Christ, the Son of God. It is the grace of God pouring in upon this world, including sinful you and sinful me.

Let us come to the table at the Eucharist with our empty hands, our child-like hands, and like little William Lawrence, let God take us in his arms and bless us.

Trinity Sunday: Father's Day

I heard a lovely tale the other day about a woman who had just turned one-hundred years old. As you might guess, there was a reporter at her door before lunch. He asked the usual questions about her life-style, what she had done or not done to live to be a hundred. The woman said, "I don't know. I just woke up this morning, and I was a hundred years old." The reporter had about the same success in asking her about her diet, about exercise, etc. It was just sort of going nowhere. Finally, he changed the subject and asked if she went to church. She said, "Of course, I go to church. I'm Episcopalian!" The reporter said, "Well, okay, but that's sometimes due to just how we were brought up. What would you be if you weren't Episcopalian?" She said: "I'd be ashamed!"

Forgive the sinful pride I take in that story and my full agreement with that dear old girl. But right now, I would settle for being a Baptist, a Methodist, a Presbyterian, or, preferably, a Unitarian—those people who believe in one God at most! Because the Episcopal Church is the only one I know of that names one Sunday of the year after a *doctrine*. And that same church, God bless it, expects me and all its clergy to say something edifying about it at least once a year. Now, that would be fine if it were the doctrine of original sin. I've got that one down pat, and I can give it to you in one, brief sentence: whatever you and I do, think, or feel, no matter how good and wonderful and beautiful in its original intent, we will eventually mess it up. That's easy.

I've been a living example of it for, lo, these many years and a practicing observer in my fellow creatures.

The doctrine of the Trinity, however, isn't quite within my scope. It's not about me and my fellow creatures. It's about God and the mystery of God's very being. And for me to explain that to you would be like a little neck clam explaining to a tea-pot all about a volcano, only more impossible.

On the other hand, if any of you out there are suffering from insomnia and could really use a bit of a nap, or if any of you are all tensed up and would like to just get a really blank stare on your face and move into another zone, I will try to accommodate you:

"Now, my dears, I shall explain to you the ultimate reality of the hypostatic union and its efficacious effect on our manifold grasp of the ground of being of our Triune God, setting at naught my fear (chuckle-chuckle) that some of you may be accusing me of Thucydideanism!"

Raise your hand when you get drowsy.

But today's doctrine Sunday occurs in a wonderful coalescence of days, Trinity Sunday and Father's Day. Those of you who've been Episcopalian for a little while know that we always introduce the Lord's Prayer by saying "We are bold to say." And why do we have to be bold? Because Abba is not father; it's Daddy. Daddy.

At any rate, I'm glad if they were going to pick a doctrine, it was the doctrine of the Trinity. It beats the daylights out of The Total Depravity of Man Sunday or maybe Original Sin Sunday. I like Father, Son, and Holy Spirit Sunday. As a matter of fact, when, if you were ever confirmed in this communion, you were asked two questions and two questions only, and neither of them had anything to do with your intellectual beliefs. One we've already heard. "Do you turn to Jesus and accept him as your Savior," and you said, "I do." "Do you put your whole trust in his grace and love," and you said "I do. And then the heavens said, "Bingo. You're in." The one thing I love about this particular Episcopal church is somehow you guys have the sense that you already had been in from the very beginning, and we're just here to kind of celebrate that and glory in it, as we just did in that howling little kid in the baptism we just did.

The doctrine of the Trinity. That came about by the early Church fathers not as an attempt to define God. They were not that dumb nor were they that arrogant— God in a prayer book, God in a bottle, God in my hip pocket because of what I think about him. Right? Wrong. The doctrine of the Trinity has more to do with us than it has with God. It has to do with the various ways we perceive him and experience his Being in our lives. God the Father. God the Creator of this fragile earth, our island home. God, the maker of the sun and stars and moons and the infinite spaces. God, whom we see somehow in sunsets and sunrises and mountains and streams and bluebirds and monkeys. That God.

I remember once my Uncle Henry who had never seen a body of water any larger than a fishing pond. My mother and sisters were gracious enough to invite their brother-in-law, my Uncle Henry, down to Jacksonville Beach, Florida. It was a long, hot trip in those days. I remember when we went across the great causeway and approached Neptune Beach, and all of a sudden, you could see the vast ocean spreading out before you, I remember Uncle Henry's comment. It sounded like he was swearing, "Great God-a-mighty. " And he was a right. Great God All Mighty.

Albert Einstein said that the most beautiful emotion in all the world is that of the mystical. It is the source, he said, of all true art and science. And the one to whom that emotion has become a stranger, who no longer wonders or stands rapt in awe, well, that man, he said, is as good as dead.

God the Creator, God the Mystery beyond us.

And then there's God the Son, God the Son of man, God the Jesus, whom we perceive in holy scripture, about whom we are told childhood tales, and in whom we hear teachings of love and mercy. As we sang it a little while ago, "Jesus, thou art all compassion / Pure unbounded love thou art." That God. His acts of healing, what he meant to those twelve and to all who knew him face to face, for whom he died and in whom he trusted, and it cost him his life. That God. The one who had the audacity to say "He who has seen me has seen the Father." That God.

And then the most mystical of all, the mystery within us, the Holy Spirit. As we call him in the creed, the "Lord and Giver of life." That God. The one whose presence we sometimes feel closer than our own hands and feet. The God we sometimes breathe as much as the air around us. That God. St. Augustine was perhaps the greatest of all teachers and writers about the doctrine of the Trinity.

121

Sometimes it got very complicated, but he would always say to his people, "Lest you become discouraged, remember that when you love you know more about who God is than you will ever know by your intellect." So there you go, Bryan Willard [the baptism of that day was Bryan Willard Chase]. We look on you, and we love you, and we love everything that gave you life and birth. And in the looking and in the longing and in the loving, we know far more about God than we deserve to know and as much about God as we need to know. For when you love, you know more about God and who he is than you will ever know otherwise.

A Happy Father's Day to you. I am touched and deeply moved by the presence of one whose father has just outrun us to the Father's house, and though we do not observe the Prayers of the People on Baptismal Day, I ask your prayers for Ed, dear, dear to Rose, and I ask your prayers for Carolyn who mourns the death of her mother Mary, and we all pray for everyone in our family who needs our care and love as we bring all of this to Abba, father, daddy.

And once more with feeling. "In the name of the Father, and of the Son, and of the Holy Spirit. Amen."

Jim's Final Sermon at St. Margaret's

From Paul's Letter to the Ephesians, the church he loved the best:

"I ask you not to lose heart over what I am suffering for you which is your glory. For this reason I bow my knees before the Father from whom every family in Heaven and on earth is named that, according to the riches of his glory, he may grant you to be strengthened with   might through his spirit in the inner person and that Christ may dwell in your hearts through faith, that you being *rooted and grounded* in love may have the power to comprehend with all saints what is the breadth and length and height and depth and to know the love of Christ which surpasses knowledge, that you may be filled with all the fullness of God."

It's presumptuous, if not preposterous, of me to take those tender and poignant words of the great Apostle. Paul wrote that letter from prison. His suffering was hard-core reality, palpable and unbearable, and he bore the marks of that sufferings upon his person as well as in his heart. It was clearly apparent.

I speak to you out of the comfort and warmth and strength and loving support of your outrageous generosity, your great unspeakable kindness to me and to Peg. So I have no right to quote Paul's words. In those wonderful words of the Bishop of Durham, "Wherever St. Paul went, he stirred up rebellion and furor; wherever I go, they serve tea."

Yeah, that's about right. You not only served tea—you served grace and love and generosity beyond words. And I speak to you out of that.

I speak to you also out of something that I found here the first day I showed up. I think it's part of the culture of this part of the world and during these times the kind of built in respect that we offer, the honor and esteem we have for, "the clergy." I didn't deserve it then, and I don't now. That's unfair. We are sinners just like the rest of us, only probably moreso. Especially when we begin to think that respect and honor is our rightful due and we become self-absorbed in our own piety and in our own importance. God help us.

Sometimes, you have been so gracious to me in your words of generosity that I hear this inner voice saying, 'If you only knew." Now what really hurts is when Peg overhears you say it, and she comes right out and says out loud, "If you only knew." Now that hurts!

Nevertheless, here we all are. And I hate to tell you that in one way or another, I've been working on this sermon for about seventy-two years. So forgive me if you're a little late getting to the Burger King.

[looking at the huge crowd] In fact, I believe there's been a terrible mistake. The Green Stamps are to be given *next* Sunday, not this.

Yes, here we all are, and my daily prayer has long been that what has been established between and among us transcends all the traditional baggage of clergy and laity, of the anointed and the anesthetized, of wacky old Father

Bubba, his song and dance, his show time, and his affinity for town drunks, and you, his long-suffering, captive crew.

There are several segments of the population that I would sort of like to address myself to. The staff, God knows the staff, this choir, this Dr. Coe, this Kathy Coe, and Ronnie and Pam and the whole crowd. You may not know this. We, because of them, are the best kept secret in the diocese of Atlanta. And I am ashamed that I have tried to keep it that way because I don't want them coming over here and messing with us. On the other hand, they are just absolutely wonderful . Their music has meant everything to me and I know to you.

And then there's Barry [Staples]. God knows there is Barry—our lay outreach minister. When I came here, I discovered to my unspeakable joy a band of ne'er-do-wells that had a little group called People for People, and they wanted to share that responsibility with me; whenever they found somebody in need, they would get together, raise a few bucks, and then they would send an anonymous cashier's check or whatever that person needed. It was then that I began to know about the heart of St. Margaret's, the kind of care you have for the poor and the disenfranchised and the lonely and those, as the prayer book says, who have none to care for them. But you cared for them. We all did. And you gave generously to their relief and, understand this, my dears, we did this out of warm hearts but at a sort of, you know, safe distance. And so have I. It's easy to write out a check and to say all the right words, "God Bless You." All that stuff. But to get face to face with their realities takes a lot of guts. And that's what old Barry has—and to spare.

And she has been the Christ to more sad people than you and I could ever imagine. I give thanks to God for her, and I ask you to do the same.

And then Paula [Pendarvis], the magician. A few years ago we were all a little bit, perhaps unfairly to ourselves, but a little bit embarrassed by our youth program because it barely existed. Now it does, and it flourishes, and it draws beautiful wonderful young people together in a way in which they come to love each other and themselves and love the way God made them. Magic. And I am grateful for that.

And then there's Julie [Foreman]. Ha-ha. Julie. I'm sorry to share this with you, if it weren't for Julie, my dears, I would most likely be in jail, okay?! She is the proverbial wind beneath my proverbial tattered old wings. And she keeps things organized. I remember people coming here long ago and saying "Father Callahan, I'm not all that . . . I've gotta tell you . . . I'm not all that interested in organized religion." And I was free to say, "Well, honey, you've found the right place. We're about as disorganized as you can get, ok."

And then along came Marion, Momma, and then right on her footsteps, her daughter Julie. And since then, we may not have been a lot of things, but we've been organized. And because of Julie I'm ashamed to tell you I've been practicing retirement now for about a year! God help me.

And then there are the lay readers and the altar guild and God only knows how many others I don't even know how to thank, but I'd like to address one group in particular.

And it's those of you who were here when I came. Those who held the fort and turned it into a beautiful and bidding home. You guys who had to choose between paying the light bill or the church mortgage or the vicar when there were hardly funds enough to pay any of them. You guys. I remember an old friend of mine. He and I were roommates in seminary. He was a Methodist preacher. He was a little tougher on sinners than I am, and he had this favorite story he liked to tell down at his church to lay out as much guilt as he could about the people who didn't come to church. I tried to say, "Bill, they ain't gonna be there to hear it." But he would still—he would still lay it out. And it goes like this.

It was a story that comes out of the second century before Christ, and it has to do with that strategic Greek city called Thermopylae. It was the boiling point of many great and decisive conflicts, but in the second century before Christ, the year 191 B.C., there was a Roman soldier whose name escapes me, and he did battle with Antiochus III, a Syrian invader. He got word from one of his centurions who had called in and feigned illness—was sorry but he "wouldn't be able to make the battle." And when the battle was over and blood had been shed and Romans and Syrians both died like flies, the General sent this message to the centurion, "We met the enemy at Thermopylae. And we conquered . And *you* were not there."

Well, you guys *were there*. And if it hadn't been for you, we wouldn't be *here*. Okay? So from the bottom of my heart, I give thanks to you.

That's why I bristle when well-meaning people say to me they're not too sure which church we are:

[in falsetto voice], "Oh yes, oh yes, Father Callahan, that precious *little* church on Newnan Street next to the funeral home. Yes, yes."

And I want to say,

"No, no, no, no, not really. I've had it checked out with builders. That *little* church weighs four hundred and sixty thousand tons. Don't let it fall on you! Also, on a big Sunday it seats about fourteen times the number of disciples our Lord started out with, and it has about four hundred sixty thousand cubic feet of space. And more than that, it is adorned with the sweat and the blood and the tears of courageous men and women and children who gave a damn. Not to mention the noble army of the martyrs."

Yeah, that church. That's the one.

And then there are the latecomers, including me. It's very significant to me that this is the first Sunday after the Epiphany—yesterday, January 6—the day that celebrates the Magi, the Wise Men. Down in south Georgia, with our dialect, we thought they were actually firemen, since according to Matthew, "They came from *afar.*" And in a way, that's not too far off the mark. They followed a fire— a bright, blazing star that shone in the east and led them to the Light of the World, the Light that shines in the darkness, yours and mine. They are also the Patron Saints of Latecomers. They showed up after the opening hymns had been sung. Moreover, they brought with them exotic gifts, not just "gold, frankincense and myrrh" but their own exotic selves, adding to the mix of the Holy Family, spicing the place up, as it were, making it the Holy Family of all Mankind. The latecomers—I give thanks to God for you.

Now I'd like to leave you a few parting shots. I'd like you to try if you can and remember the things that, at least it seems to me, I was led by God to say to you. And the first has to do with the wonderful passage from Saint Luke that we've read, the baptism of Jesus. We paint it with pretty pictures. We sometimes forget it was kind of a messy scene. The Jews believed that the sins of the sinners washed off into the water of baptism. So there they all were, the whores, the Pharisees, the Publicans, the generals, the run of the mill of your ordinary day-by-day sinner, there they all were, and finally there he stood right in the midst of their sins. And he was *glad* to be there.

And I remember, of course, a story no one else but John Porter could have told me. In a seminar course on the Old Testament, the seminar teacher was the great Diedrich Reich, and at the conclusion of the course, Diedrich Reich asked them all if they could say in a few words what they thought to be the very essence of the teaching of the Old Testament. And they all volunteered the sort of superficial things, God's justice, God's mercy, and old Professor Wright sort of shook his head, waiting so he could tell them what he wanted to tell them in the first place. "The essence of the Old Testament is that God is not afraid to dirty his hands in the filth and the mire of the world." Remember that.

Another thing I'd sort of like to remind you of—is you've heard it too many times but maybe you've forgotten it—that Jesus did not come to improve the improvable, or reward the rewardable, or to purify the impure, or to punish the punishable. He came to raise the dead! He came to raise us dead!

I have a few instructions for you now. When I was a wet-behind-the-ears Methodist preacher, I went to St. Simon's Island, to Epworth-by-the-Sea, to hear the great English Methodist, a man named William E. Sangster. I'll hope you'll remember this drill because you're going to be called on it before this morning's service is over. He had a wonderful sermon that he called "Three Cheers."

"Be of good cheer," Jesus said to the paralytic, "Your sins are forgiven." To those bewildered disciples out on the stormy sea, "Be of good cheer. It is I. Be not afraid." Finally, to his devastated disciples, as they said their parting words, he said, "In the world you shall have tribulation, but be of good cheer. I have overcome the world."

And then this old British geezer said, "Therefore, I say to you. Three cheers for Jesus!" And nobody did anything. I wanted to get up and yell, "Give me a J! Give me an E." Well, I made you this promise a good many months ago, and I'm gonna keep it. We're leaving today not with the lovely, little, pious "Let us go in peace to serve the Lord." We're leaving today with, and you know the drill, "Hip, Hip . . ." [here, some child in the crowd yells out "Hooray," and Jim says, "No, not yet. We have dignified things to do first!"]. I will tell you this. I've been in this ministry a long time now. I've never ex-communicated anyone. But if you don't say "Hooray" to my "Hip, Hip," consider yourself ex-communicado, okay?

And the last reminder comes from an old rock group that you may remember. They had a wonderful name, America, and they sang this little song.

"Oz never did give nothing to the tin man that the tin man didn't already have."

Precisely. I've never brought you anything or given you anything that you didn't already have and that you, without knowing it, had given to me. Now if I have at all awakened in you that which you already had, then as my mama would say, sometimes sarcastically, "Pin a rose on me." But know it for what is. Know that it's all about you. It's all about us. And includes most of all the One who never ever leaves us.

You remember that.

And remember me.

Lisa Plummer Crafton

28240296R00080

Made in the USA
Charleston, SC
05 April 2014